99)

WOMAN OF STRENGTH

Woman of Strength

LEARNING FROM THE
PROVERBS 31 WOMAN

servant

AN IMPRINT OF
FRANCISCAN MEDIA
Cincinnati, Ohio

Cover and book design by Mark Sullivan
Cover image © Kelly Marken | Fotolia

Library of Congress Cataloging-in-Publication Data
Woman of strength : learning from the Proverbs 31 woman / editors of Servant Books.
pages cm
Includes bibliographical references.
ISBN 978-1-61636-905-7 (alk. paper)
1. Christian women—Religious life. 2. Bible. Proverbs—Meditations. I. Servant Books
(Firm)
BV4527.W5865 2015
248.8'43—dc23
2014037897

ISBN 978-1-61636-905-7

Published by Servant, an imprint of
Franciscan Media
28 W. Liberty St.
Cincinnati, OH 45202
www.FranciscanMedia.org

Printed in the United States of America.
Printed on acid-free paper.
15 16 17 18 19 5 4 3 2 1

Contents

Proverbs 31

Who can find a good wife?
   She is far more precious than jewels.
The heart of her husband trusts in her,
   and he will have no lack of gain.
She does him good, and not harm,
   ]all the days of her life.
She seeks wool and flax,
   and works with willing hands.
She is like the ships of the merchant,
   she brings her food from afar.
She rises while it is yet night
   and provides food for her household
   and tasks for her maidens.
She considers a field and buys it;
   with the fruit of her hands she plants a vineyard.
She clothes her loins with strength
   and makes her arms strong.
She perceives that her merchandise is profitable.
   Her lamp does not go out at night.
She puts her hands to the distaff,
   and her hands hold the spindle.
She opens her hand to the poor,
   and reaches out her hands to the needy.
She is not afraid of snow for her household,
   for all her household are clothed in scarlet.
She makes herself coverings;
   her clothing is fine linen and purple.

Her husband is known in the gates,
  when he sits among the elders of the land.
She makes linen garments and sells them;
  she delivers girdles to the merchant.
Strength and dignity are her clothing,
  and she laughs at the time to come.
She opens her mouth with wisdom,
  and the teaching of kindness is on her tongue.
She looks well to the ways of her household,
  and does not eat the bread of idleness.
Her children rise up and call her blessed;
  her husband also, and he praises her:
"Many women have done excellently,
  but you surpass them all."
Charm is deceitful, and beauty is vain,
  but a woman who fears the LORD is to be praised.
Give her of the fruit of her hands,
  and let her works praise her in the gates.

—PROVERBS 31:10–31

Preface

At first reading, the advice Proverbs 31 gives might intimidate us. Where does this godly woman find time for everything? How did she become so skilled? Does she ever sleep?

Is this advice relevant to our times? How many of us weave our own fabrics or make clothes for our whole household? We seldom are in a position to buy and sell land, though women do seem to excel as realtors. Many of us wish we had "maidens" to whom we could "provide tasks"!

Though the applications have changed, Proverbs 31 is very inspiring for today's Christian woman. We see in this passage the characteristics necessary to live the Christian life: diligence, wisdom, strength, generosity, trust in God, joy, respect, and kindness. These qualities will never go out of date.

Over the past several years, Servant has published many books that give women encouragement and direction on how to live for God. Here we are pleased to offer selections from some of those books. We hope these adaptations—along with the added Scripture passages and prayers at the beginnings and ends of them—will aid you in your journey toward everyday holiness.

Many of the authors cited here are "Proverbs 31 women." Some are wives and mothers who offer both practical and spiritual advice on how to lovingly serve our families. Some are spiritual mothers. God has abundantly gifted them all, and they use those gifts to bless others.

Other chapters come from those whom we might call "Proverbs 31 men and children." They "praise" some of the holy women of history, such as St. Thérèse of Lisieux and Mother Teresa of Calcutta. They "rise up to call blessed" the women of God who have aided their journey to holiness.

Our hope in presenting this book is that all Christian women will continue to grow in the practices and virtues that life for God requires. May we work diligently for his kingdom, and may our hope in him be so constant that we can "laugh at the time to come."

Introduction

God walks among the pots and pans.

—St. Teresa of Avila

On many occasions, the late Pope John Paul II reminded the Church of the universal call to holiness. "Everyone in the Church," he wrote, "precisely because they are members, receive and thereby share in the common vocation to holiness."[1] The Second Vatican Council put it this way:

> All Christians in any state or walk of life are called to the fullness of Christian life and to the perfection of love.

> This holiness, the council said, grows out of giving glory to God, serving others, and "doing the will of God in everything.[2]

But what is holiness, and how do we respond to the call? Can we do the will of God *in everything?*

St. Benedict, the founder of monasticism in Europe, wrote that the keeper of the pots, pans, and "all utensils and goods of the monastery" should regard them as "sacred vessels of the altar."[3] The holiness of pots and pans points to the holiness of everyday life. The things we do in everyday life lead us to holiness if we do them with an awareness of the presence of God.

In seeking to grow spiritually, we might sometimes think that we need something big to happen. While dramatic changes have often accompanied spiritual growth, holiness does not always take big steps. "The older I get," Dorothy Day wrote, "the more I see that life is made up of many steps, and they are very small affairs, not giant strides."[4] Little steps work just as well as big ones, sometimes better.

Thérèse of Lisieux, Dorothy Day, and Mother Teresa found their vocations to be made up of small things: serving the "little ones" of God; doing small, everyday acts of faith, hope, and love over and over again; pouring love and devotion into everything they did—in short, seeing the connection between the ordinary activities of life and the presence of God. Why should the everyday tasks of life reveal the divine any less than larger and more dramatic spiritual gestures do?

The world tends to measure success and effectiveness in terms of big numbers: how much money someone makes, how much a person owns, how much they accomplish, and so on. Today's generation of women seems to be asking, "Can we really have it all? And if we can, do we really *want* it?" Even as the lives of women are more varied and creatively rich than at any other time in human history, our myriad of choices come with an equal number of distractions. The more responsibilities we have, the more potential stress we have. The more roles we play, the less likely we are to truly know ourselves.

Even with the world as our oyster, so to speak, and with no limits to what we can become, women's sphere of influence still begins with our families and extends out into the world like so many concentric circles or ripples in a pond. And yes, sometimes that pond feels like an ocean when it comes to sorting through everything that needs to get done!

Some women have made the choice to stay at home. Some are choosing to home school. Some women are raising and supporting children on their own. Others, though fulfilled by motherhood, see the value in also pursuing a profession that utilizes their gifts and talents outside the home. Still other women are not called to physical motherhood but instead take on the role of spiritual mother in the Church or in the community in which they live. And finally, we can't forget the women in our midst who are godmothers, grandmothers, and great-grandmothers.

Each woman has a vital role to play in the kingdom. And God has something to say to each concerning that role.

—JOEL SCHORN AND ANNE COSTA

More Precious Than Jewels

What is your beloved more than another beloved,
O fairest among women?

—Song of Solomon 5:9

St. Teresa Benedicta of the Cross believed that before we can carry out our specific roles and fulfill our God-given vocations, we need to first become a person!

Before a woman can become wife and mother in a positive way, she must first mature in her own self-possession. Although woman longs to love and receive love, she must also become strong enough to be a true gift to another.

—*Anne Costa*

❧ WHAT REALLY COUNTS ❧

Beloved, we are God's children now.

—1 JOHN 3:2

The word for *jewels* in Hebrew refers to something very costly, like rubies or pearls. Proverbs 31 tells us that these pale in comparison to the value of a godly wife.

In Matthew 13:45–46, Jesus tells about a man who finds a pearl of great price in a field owned by someone else. He puts it back in the ground and then sells everything he has to purchase that field and possess the pearl. The pearl to which Jesus refers is the Gospel, worth any price. The Church, possessing the Gospel, is a bride of inestimable worth. A similar understanding can be applied to a godly wife: She is worth any amount of sacrifice to her husband and children.

Who or what determines our value? If we look to our present culture, we get one set of answers; if we look to the Lord, we get a very different answer. The world judges us on appearances; God judges the heart.

External criteria include youthfulness, beauty, talent, skill, wealth, intelligence, and fame. Though certain individuals excel in these areas, even the "winners" know they stand on shaky ground.

Those with youth or beauty know that it is just a matter of time before someone younger or more beautiful garners attention. Even pageant queens can list flaws they would correct to be more attractive. One attractive but aging actress wondered if she had the courage to refuse plastic surgery.

Those with money constantly compare themselves to others with more. How much is enough to be satisfied or to feel secure?

Those with fame—for their skill, talent, or physical prowess—wonder how long they will remain in the limelight. And though the rich and famous may appear happy, the papers are replete with stories of their loneliness and isolation.

For some, it is not beauty or brawn that defines them but their brains that establish their sense of worth. They pursue higher levels of education and seek career advancement and its monetary rewards. Yet they know that younger people willing to be paid less for the same job are in line waiting for their opportunity. Eventually retirement comes, and then what is left of an identity so closely associated with mental acuity and job performance?

Even marital status can give a false sense of value. Perhaps a woman remains single to prove she does not need a man, only to end up lonely. Or a woman marries in search of an identity, only to discover a sense of loss or abandonment instead of fulfillment. Though our spouses and children should *affirm* our worth, they do not *determine* our worth.

In stark contrast to all of these ways to measure our value, God speaks to the hearts of his beloved daughters and sons. He says, "You are precious because I made you and redeemed you. I give you your sense of worth."

Lord, thank you for your great love for me. I rest in that love; I delight in that love; I want only more of that love.

—*Kimberly Hahn*

CROWN OF CREATION

> I praise you, for I am wonderfully made.
> Wonderful are your works!
>
> —PSALM 139:14, *NAB*

In the very first book of the Bible, Genesis, we find the account of how God created the world out of nothing. He created the earth, wind, sea and sky, plants and animals, rocks and trees. After each new creation, he stepped back to look at what he had just made and said, "This is good" (see Genesis 1).

As his final act, God created humans in his own image and likeness. When God created the parents of the human race as a reflection of his own image, he was not just creating a superior model of animal. He made us *different* from all other creatures, because each person, male or female, has a *spirit* that is like his Spirit.

When God looked at that couple he had just created, he said, "This is very good" (see Genesis 1:31). Did you catch that? The man and the woman had done absolutely *nothing* yet. All they had done was to *be*. They stood in God's presence without any expectations to offer him or the world. Without having accomplished anything at all, they were declared "very good" simply because they had been created by God. They were *that* good.

We humans are created in God's image and likeness, and he has never changed his mind about us. We have absolutely everything within us to be the men and women he made us to be. And that is very, very good. *We* are very, very good.

I do not want to argue about how we were created or how we all evolved or when it all happened. My focus is God's place in our creation. God intervened, and we became like him. At some point, God's breath (see Genesis 2:7) was breathed into us, and we became human.

As women we are part of that creation, part of that "good" God talks about. In fact, the only time during Creation that God did not say that something was good was when he said, "It is not good for man to be alone"—and so he created woman (see Genesis 2:18). We are complete as male and female, and *that* is good!

Woman—the final creation in God's masterpiece of creation. No wonder Pope John Paul II so often referred to the man and woman that God created in his final genesis act as "the crown of creation"![5] Women are like the finishing strokes of vibrant color on a masterpiece, the all-important details that bring life to the work of art.

Somewhere along the way, we lost sight of the gift of "good" we bring to the world simply by being God's creation. I don't think we wanted to lose sight; I think we just forgot. We forgot that what other people think of us or say about us doesn't change us. We forgot that our beauty cannot be measured by pounds, wrinkles, hairstyles, or clothing. We forgot that our value is determined by the same endlessly creative One who created the earth, wind, sea, sky, rainbows, mountains, sunsets, and snow, whose knowledge of beauty is greater than we can imagine and whose expressions of love to the world are more than we can fathom.

He made *you*. And then he said, without hesitation or second-guessing, "This is very good." That statement remains true no matter what life circumstances come your way.

Lord, thank you for making me "very good"! I delight in being your creation and your beloved.

—*Tammy Evevard*

Husbands, love your wives, as Christ loved the church and
gave himself up for her, that he might sanctify her.

—EPHESIANS 5:25–26

The cross is the consummation—the complete enactment in the
flesh—of God's eternal covenant of love with his people. In pouring
out his life for us, the Son of God espoused the Church in an irrevo-
cable bond. His gift is radical and total; it is all that God could give of
himself to man.

The essence of the love of a husband is to lay down his life for his
bride. What then is the essence of a wife's response? To *receive* that love
with complete openness and *return* it with a reciprocal gift of self. Only
when the gift is reciprocated is there a spousal union. Only when we
recognize Jesus's act of love on the cross for what it is and respond to it
in gratitude and love, is our covenant bond with him made complete.
The Church "completes [the sacrament of Christ's redemption] just as
the wife, in virtue of spousal love, completes her husband."[6]

The covenant between husband and wife is consummated and
renewed in their physical union: The two become one flesh. Analogously,
the Eucharist is the consummation and renewal of Christ's spousal gift
of himself on the cross. It is his one-flesh union with his Church. Each
time we consume the Eucharist, we are invited to enter into personal
"communion" with Christ, to receive his total gift of himself into the
depths of our heart and respond by giving ourselves to him in love and
gratitude.

The spousal analogy holds true not only for the Church as a whole but for each of us as individuals, both men and women. Pope John Paul II says:

> All human beings—both women and men—are called through the Church, to be the "Bride" of Christ. The God who "first loved us" (1 John 4:19) and did not hesitate to deliver his Son out of love (see John 3:16) impels the Church to go "all the way" (see John 13:1) in love. And she is called to do so with the freshness of two spouses who love each other in the joy of giving themselves without reserve and in daily generosity.[7]

A spousal love for God does not preclude our having a human spouse. But it is a love that is total, that involves the surrender of our entire being.

The ultimate model of a bridal response to God is the Virgin Mary. When the angel Gabriel came to her at the Annunciation, she said: "*Fiat*," "Let it be to me according to your word" (Luke 1:38). More than any other human being, Mary received the gift of God with complete openness, availability, and gratitude. And her spousal communion with God was so total and so fruitful that she conceived and brought forth into the world the Son of God himself.

In an analogous way, we are all called to conceive God, to make room for him in our hearts. We are to say with Paul, "It is no longer I who live, but Christ who lives in me" (Galatians 2:20). In so doing we become, like Mary, a *theotokos*, a God-bearer.

To live this truth means to recognize that holiness is not something I *do* but something I *receive*. This truth is liberating! It takes the pressure off and frees us from the treadmill of religious self-effort. To deny this truth, on the other hand, leads to an overemphasis on programs and activities. We can organize all kinds of efforts "for Christ" without bothering to sit at his feet and receive what he actually wants to give. This severely limits our spiritual fruitfulness.

It should be noted that receptivity is not at all the same as passivity. Receptivity actually engages all our energy. It takes just as much skill for the running back to catch the football as for the quarterback to throw it. To listen well to a speaker involves just as much energy, attention, and thought as does speaking. The more we, as members of the Church, become receptive to the immensity of love God pours out on us, the more we become spiritually fruitful. Through us, others are able to be born into and mature in God's family.

Lord, thank you for making me your bride. I devote myself to loving you completely. Mary, help me be a bride worthy of your son.

Hail, Holy Queen, Mother of Mercy, our life, our sweetness and our hope.
To thee do we cry, poor banished children of Eve.
To thee do we send up our sighs, mourning and weeping in this valley of tears.
Turn then, most gracious advocate, thine eyes of mercy toward us;
and after this our exile, show unto us the blessed fruit of thy womb, Jesus.
O clement, O loving, O sweet Virgin Mary.
Pray for us, most holy Mother of God,
that we may be made worthy of the promises of Christ.

—Mary Healy

⧉ Choosing Beauty ⧉

A woman's beauty gladdens the countenance, and surpasses
every human desire.

—Sirach 36:22

Scripture says that of all the things human beings crave, women's
beauty tops the list. And our experience supports the idea. We place a
high value on feminine beauty: men love to behold it, and women long
to have it.

Why did God make women especially beautiful? Why did he plant
a desire for feminine beauty in the hearts of men and women alike?

I believe he did this as a way to reveal himself to us. In the divine
design, a woman's beauty—her true, authentic beauty—is a gateway to
God. Ultimately, the thirst for beauty is a thirst for God himself.

I'm not talking about the one-dimensional beauty of the airbrushed
supermodels on the covers of *Glamour* and *Vogue*, mind you. I'm talking
about the built-in beauty—both physical and spiritual—of *every*
woman, you and me included. We were made in the image of God
precisely as women. In its fullness, our beauty is a reflection of our
Creator, the perfect artist who defines beauty itself. Our true beauty
shines most clearly when we live in harmony with him.

Holiness embellishes our inborn beauty as nothing else can. And
this fullness of beauty is freely accessible to everyone. It is all up to us:
We can choose to let this beauty flourish, or we can ignore the primary
importance of our spiritual life and settle for mediocre, worldly beauty
alone.

Scripture gives us a picture of a woman who is the perfect blend
of spiritual and physical beauty. These verses speak in the context of
marriage, but the ideals apply to all women:

Like the sun rising in the heights of the Lord,
   so is the beauty of a good wife in her well-ordered home.
Like the shining lamp on the holy lampstand,
   so is a beautiful face on a stately figure.
Like pillars of gold on a base of silver,
   so are beautiful feet with a steadfast heart. (Sirach 26:16–18)

The beauty of a virtuous woman lights up her home, her community, her workplace, "like the sun." She is inherently attractive. This is exactly what so many women long to be. And this longing to be attractive, beautiful even, is planted in our hearts by God. He made us to be beautiful in the fullest sense, inside and out.

Lord, you have made me beautiful. You have crowned me with glory and honor (Psalm 8:5). I choose to allow your beauty to shine in me. Let it flourish, Lord, that I may be your spotless bride.

—Gina Loehr

❧ WRAPPED IN GOD'S ARMS ❧

Those who drink of the water that I will give them will never
be thirsty. The water that I will give will become in them a
spring of water gushing up to eternal life.

—JOHN 4:14, *NRSV*

The Samaritan woman who met Jesus at the well (see John 4:1–42)
wasn't expecting company that day. She certainly never would have
expected to enter into a deep conversation with a man, particularly a
Jewish man. Men and women did not relate to each other the way we
relate today. In addition, Samaritans were not a "pure" race and were
therefore considered "unclean" by the Jews.

On top of the huge class division issue was the matter of this
woman's lifestyle. The man she was living with was not her husband—
something quite scandalous in those days. And she also had a long and
colorful history with men.

At the end of her encounter with Jesus, however, the woman leaves
her water jug and her low confidence behind. She has found the living
water. She runs all over town, eagerly looking for the people whom she
previously went to great lengths to avoid. She is forever changed and
wants to tell everyone about her experience (see John 4:28–29, 39–41).

Many of us can identify with the Samaritan woman: We hide from
or fail to recognize our own dignity and worth. It is much easier to
keep going back to the same old well rather than break out of our
normal routine and burst forth with joy and fruitfulness. Too many of
us settle, just as the Samaritan woman did. We allow our imperfections
and mistakes to limit us to the status quo.

In the twenty-first century, reasons why we should hold back are heaped upon us continuously. Criticisms and comparisons brought on by an out-of-control culture combined with our own endless mind games, mistakes, or serious sins can leave us frozen or paralyzed.

With this in mind, let's take a look at what the Catholic Church had to say to women nearly fifty years ago, words that are quite prophetic. The closing speech of the Second Vatican Council was given on December 8, 1965, on the Feast of the Immaculate Conception, a very important holy day in the Catholic Church. The closing statement appears even more profound given the tumultuous climate of the 1960s.

> But the hour is coming, in fact has come, when the vocation of woman is being achieved in its fullness, the hour in which woman acquires in the world an influence, an effect and a power never hitherto achieved. That is why, at this moment when the human race is undergoing so deep a transformation, women impregnated with the spirit of the Gospel can do so much to aid mankind in not falling.[8]

One of the rules I have learned about Scripture in my many years of Bible study is that not one word is ever wasted. In the case of the Samaritan woman, the lessons are many, and they are deep. Of course Jesus wanted to save this woman from herself and give her everlasting life. He also wanted to show us women of today that we are truly gifts and that he loves us just because we are his. If we could just start there, wrapping ourselves up in his arms, resting as the Samaritan woman did in that one amazing fact that she was loved by God! If we could only realize that we are gifts, the hand that rocks the cradle would not only rule the world but save it from itself. Pope Paul VI said:

You women have always had as your lot the protection of the home, the love of beginnings and an understanding of cradles. You are present in the mystery of a life beginning. You offer consolation in the departure of death. Our technology runs the risk of becoming inhuman. Reconcile men with life and above all, we beseech you, watch carefully over the future of our race. Hold back the hand of man, who, in a moment of folly might attempt to destroy human civilization.[9]

Dear God, I reject the false standards of today's culture that bombard me. Help me rise above my feelings and imperfections and embrace my God-given dignity. Wrapped in the arms of Jesus, I want to share the gift of myself freely and confidently with those around me.

—Teresa Tomeo

Called to Love

What can a person do who tries to love God tremendously? Everything, from putting the lights off, to refraining from changing clothes every five minutes, to being indifferent to food, to going wherever God calls you. Once I know God's will, I am going to try to do it perfectly. My heart swells and I say, "This also, Lord, for love of you."... It never occurs to me that I can possibly separate anything from love. Wherever you go you will certainly have to do little things. Try to do them without love, and see what happens. But doing little things with our whole hearts is our vocation. (Catherine de Hueck Doherty)

—Debra Herbeck

A SINCERE GIFT

This is my commandment, that you love one another as I have loved you.

—JOHN 15:12

Surely, the logical, mundane response to suffering is to refuse to love. Whether because of dysfunction within the family or unfortunate encounters with others, many girls learn early in life to protect their hearts by limiting their generosity. They set up a host of inconsistent boundaries that have less to do with virtue than with survival. Even in intimate encounters and within their families, many are afraid to give a complete gift of self. Through this very caution, they cut themselves off from the only guaranteed avenue of happiness. Their need for love and stability doesn't diminish; their greatest desires are thwarted by confusion over where and how to expend their energy, and each step in their disordered search for intimacy only deepens the spiral of pain.

The crux of the matter is that man and woman are both called to generous love, to complete gifts of self, but precisely because women are icons of the Church—the paradigm of the feminine responsiveness that ultimately includes all of creation—they must be first to model this love. Pope John Paul II wrote in his apostolic letter "On the Dignity and Vocation of Women":

> "Man, who is the only creature on earth that God willed for its own sake, cannot fully find himself except through a sincere gift of self." This applies to every human being, as a person created in God's image, whether man or woman. This ontological affirmation also indicates the ethical dimension of a

person's vocation. *Woman can only find herself by giving love to others.*[10]

That means that, despite the fallen world, despite their particular vulnerabilities, and despite the pain involved, it is essential that women persevere in love. They must love for two reasons: The world needs their love, and their own happiness depends upon it. Who but women have been invited to receive human persons and to form them through the multifaceted gift of motherhood?

The fact that the spiritual and emotional health of each woman has a profound rippling effect on the wider culture cannot be overstated. It is for this very reason that there was an urgent call to women included in the Closing Documents of the Second Vatican Council: "[A]t this moment when the human race is undergoing so deep a transformation, women impregnated with the spirit of the Gospel can do so much to aid mankind in not falling."[11]

So what does the "spirit of the Gospel" tell us about loving in a fallen world? The answer is clear: We are to forgive the injuries and love those who have harmed us. The Bridegroom himself came in love and was crucified, and his last words were words of forgiveness (see Luke 23:34, 43). As icons of his beloved bride, we have no other option, despite the staggering implications of such a demand.

Lord, you are my Bridegroom, and so I give my all to you. I want to love and forgive as you do. Fill me with your own love and mercy for all whom I encounter.

—*Genevieve Kineke*

❧ REAL LOVE ☙

In this is love, not that we loved God but that he loved us and
sent his Son to be the expiation for our sins.

—1 JOHN 4:10

I am not a romantic, I am a realist, and yet I think about love all the
time. Love is what gives my life direction and purpose. Love shapes
my actions and guides my words; it gets me out of bed in the morning
and helps me sleep at night. Love tells me who I am and helps me see
others as they really are.

Love is real. At the center of this reality is a divine Person, the source
of all human love whose outstretched arms show me what true love
looks like. This immense love is deeper and wider than the whole
universe, yet it stoops low to enter my poor soul and ignite a flame
within me that will burn forever.

Real love is necessary for real life. Real love shows up not only in
times of great joy, delight, and fulfillment but especially when life seems
overwhelming and incomprehensible, filled with unbearable suffering
and sorrow. It is in these times that love has shown me the way, not
around the pain but through it. Love is stronger than death.

Many years ago, I asked God to fill me with his love and teach me
what it truly means to love. Every day I try to say yes to loving the
person God gives me in that moment—my husband, a family member,
a friend, a coworker, a stranger, an adversary, even myself. If I can string
together these moments of love, then perhaps my life can be a reflection of God's great love.

God is all love. This gentle Savior pleads with us from the
Host: "Love Me as I have loved you; abide in My love! I came

to cast the fire of My love on the earth, and My most ardent desire is that it should set your hearts on fire."

—St. Peter Julian Eymard[12]

Dear Lord, let the fire of your love burn in me! Let it be an inextinguishable flame that lights my life, purifies my heart, and directs my actions.

—*Debra Herbeck*

❧ Expansive Souls ❧

If you utter what is precious, and not what is worthless,
you shall be as my mouth.

—Jeremiah 15:19

An expansive soul is one that is open to all human beings and is inclusive and championing of all life as sacred, God-given, and of infinite worth. It is a soul that is primarily concerned with human relationships and the dignity of the human person. Women are uniquely equipped to care for, nurture, and continually cultivate life and life-giving connections and relationships among human beings. We are wired to foster these connections, not just on a person-to-person level but to build bridges within our families, at our workplaces, and in our communities. No matter what our sphere of influence, our expansive souls are particularly attuned to make right the wrongs of exclusivity, divisiveness, dehumanization, or destruction within relationships.

Given this, we can understand the important influence that women can have on our culture and in our societies. If each woman cultivated expansiveness within her soul, the fabric of our society would be knitted together much more tightly than it is today, and the strength of the bonds that women inherently nurture would bring back sanity and structure to our families and our world. Pope John Paul II said in his apostolic letter to women:

> The moral and spiritual strength of a woman is joined to her awareness that *God entrusts the human being to her in a special way*. Our time in particular *awaits the manifestation* of that

"genius" which belongs to women, and which can ensure sensitivity for human beings in every circumstance.[13]

Woman's awareness of her expansive soul needs to be heightened, because when it is compromised, misunderstood, or disregarded altogether, she can fall prey to what Edith Stein refers to as an "unchecked need for communication."[14] This includes a tendency toward disingenuous curiosity and entanglement in relationships that are superficial and self-serving. It can lead us to become involved in and concerned about relationships only as a means for gossip or as a means to exert our own will upon others.

I have to be honest and admit that this is something I struggle with on a daily basis! I find that it can take an almost supernatural self-discipline to resist engaging in damaging conversations with others. One of the ways I try to combat this, besides going to frequent confession, is to make a Sign of the Cross with holy water over my lips every time I bless myself as I am leaving church. It's a reminder to me of what we are told in the Scriptures, that the tongue is like a tiny little rudder that can steer a large ship quite far from the virtuous shores! (See James 3:4–5.)

I have been blessed by the example of several strong, mentoring women who, along with God's grace, have helped me to "extinguish the wildfire of the tongue." They have not been afraid to gently but firmly offer counsel and correction when I have fallen short in this matter. We need more women of such courage who are willing to apply some influential virtue. As Edith Stein said, "For women to be shaped in accordance with their authentic nature and destiny, they must be educated by authentic women."[15]

Using our voices to edify, exhort, and encourage others can be the *positive* outpouring of an expansive soul. As women, let us make a pact to help each other rise to this ideal in all our relationships.

Lord, thank you for the expansive soul you have given me. "Set a guard over my mouth" (Psalm 141:3), that I may speak only what you wish me to say. And for all my sins in this area, I pray:

O my God, I am heartily sorry for having offended thee.

And I detest all my sins because of thy just punishments,

but most of all because they offend thee, my God,

who art all good and deserving of all my love.

I firmly resolve, with the help of thy grace,

to confess my sins, to do penance, and to amend my life. Amen.

Lord, give me wisdom in prayer, through reading your Word, and through the guidance of holy men and women.

—Anne Costa

❧ Love with Dignity ❧

And the King will answer them, "Truly, I say to you, as you did
it to one of the least of these my brethren, you did it to me."
—Matthew 25:40

St. Thomas Aquinas defined Christian love as willing the good of
another. What can we do to love those around us? What do our loved
ones, friends, and coworkers need from us? How about the other people
we encounter—those who stand behind cash registers, wait on us at
restaurants, or help us find something in a store? Do we treat them as
beloved children of God, just as we want others to treat us?

Then come those we find most difficult to love: people with whom
we are in conflict, whom we dislike, who trouble us with their inconsid-
erateness and selfishness, their bad habits or destructive behavior. Jesus
was clear about such relationships:

Love your enemies, do good to those who hate you, bless those
who curse you, pray for those who abuse you. Give to everyone
who begs from you; and if anyone takes away your goods do
not ask for them again. Do to others as you would have them
do to you. Love your enemies, do good, and lend, expecting
nothing in return. Your reward will be great. Be merciful,
just as your Father is merciful. (Luke 6:27–28, 30–31, 35, 36,
NRSV)

Whether we are dealing with the materially or the spiritually poor—
those in our homes or those outside our homes, loved ones, strangers,
or enemies—God calls us to see the dignity of every person and to take
steps to build up that dignity. For example, Mother Teresa's care for
lepers and other sick people involved not only dispensing anti-leprosy

sulfone drugs, physical treatment, and giving free rice and milk. The sisters also sought to give those in their care the dignity their situations had damaged.

Dorothy Day painted a picture of the unemployed and sick people the Catholic Workers served in their bread lines: "They are stripped then, not only of all earthly goods, but of spiritual goods, their sense of human dignity. When they are forced into line at municipal lodging houses, in clinics, in our houses of hospitality, they are then the truly destitute."[16]

The Catholic Workers sought to provide sustenance while preserving dignity. "We only tried to fulfill their immediate needs without probing, and to make them feel at home, and try to help them in regaining some measure of self-respect."[17] A jail stay later in life helped Dorothy "see how much we accomplish at The Catholic Worker by not asking questions or doing any investigating but by cultivating a spirit of trust."[18]

This desire to care for souls as well as bodies comes from an all-embracing spirituality of God's presence in oneself, in every person, rich or poor, and in the whole world. Mother Teresa did not want her sisters to be only "social workers"[19] or teachers or caregivers. Their work came from their desire to practice their faith: They were to be contemplatives in the world and prayer professionals whose mission grew out of finding God's presence in their surroundings. Mother asked the sisters to have "the constant awareness of the Divine Presence everywhere and in everyone, especially in our own hearts and in the hearts of our Sisters with whom we live, and in the poorest of the poor."[20]

Lord, you love people, not programs. Help us see people as you do. We seek your presence each day in prayer so that we may love you more deeply and honor your image in each person we meet throughout the day.

—Joel Schorn

❧ THE APOSTOLATE OF PRESENCE ☙

When Jesus saw his mother, and the disciple whom he loved
standing near, he said to his mother, "Woman, behold, your
son!" Then he said to the disciple, "Behold, your mother!"

—JOHN 19:26–27

We women have an apostolate of presence in our home. We want to
develop meaningful relationships with each family member, to treasure
our time with each one. One new mom wrote about her baby, "I am
totally, hopelessly in love with him. I want to remember every moment,
every detail, yet I already realize these times that I so carefully cherish
will be harder and harder to recall. For now I am content to keep the
rest of the world at bay, to learn his ways, and all the ways I love him
and his presence in our life."

This simple poem came to me as I pondered the wonder of my first
grandchild, Veronica Margaret, and the goodness of God through my
precious daughter-in-law, Sarah. I was reminded of my love for my
children, for my mom, and for Mother Mary:

Layers of Life-Nurturing Love

I need my mother!
Her eyes' tender gaze—not for anything I have done
but simply for who I am.
Her hands' tender touch—compassion expressed for the
little hurts that overwhelm me,
though she knows how little they are.
Her voice speaking words of love over me,
whether or not I understand what she is saying.

Her breasts combining milk I need with the milk of human kindness,
not just giving me better food but giving me herself.
Her time, unhurried, as we bask in the warmth of faithful and fruitful
love.
Her prayers enveloping me in the love of God,
so that he is the air I breathe, the atmosphere of our home.
Her being, laid down for me,
so that I have life and I live!
I need my mother!
Nana

A wife's contribution to the family is real even if it is not always as tangible as a man's paycheck. She contributes much more than a paycheck: a stable presence, a ground of being for all of the members of the family. Children do not need caregivers, super-special day-care centers, or after-school programs. They need their mom.

Lord, your love is like that of a mother—unconditional, constant, nurturing, wise. Let that love flow through me to my children and all the people you entrust to my care.

Thank you for my motherhood. Thank you for my earthly mother and all the mothers I know. And thank you for the Mother you share with us, who is always ready to strengthen and guide.

Hail Mary, full of grace, the Lord is with you.

Blessed are you among women, and blessed is the fruit of your womb, Jesus.

Holy Mary, Mother of God, pray for us sinners

now and at the hour of our death. Amen.

—*Kimberly Hahn*

Family

God created man in his own image, in the image of God he created him; male and female he created them. And God blessed them, and God said to them, "Be fruitful and multiply, and fill the earth and subdue it."

—GENESIS 1:27–28

In our own time, in a world often alien and even hostile to faith, believing families are of primary importance as centers of living, radiant faith. For this reason the Second Vatican Council, using an ancient expression, calls the family the *Ecclesia domestica* [domestic Church]. It is in the bosom of the family that parents are "by word and example...the first heralds of the faith with regard to their children. They should encourage them in the vocation which is proper to each child, fostering with special care any religious vocation."

—*CATECHISM OF THE CATHOLIC CHURCH,*

QUOTING *LUMEN GENTIUM*, 11

❧ LOVE BEGINS AT HOME ❧

Let us love one another; for love is of God, and he who loves
is born of God and knows God.

—1 JOHN 4:7

On a visit to a church in Ireland, Mother Teresa expressed her concern
about the practice of institutionalizing the vulnerable. "If you really
love God, begin by loving your child, your husband, your wife. The
old people, where are they? They are in some institution. Why are they
not with you? Where is the crippled child? In some institution. Why
is that child not with you? That child, young mothers and fathers, is a
gift from God."[21]

Love does begin at home, where we are, and in a sense it should
stay there. Mother Teresa saw this in her childhood, when her mother,
Drana, opened the family home to the poor. One elderly woman was
a regular guest for meals. Drana told her daughter: "Welcome her
warmly, with love. My child, never eat a single mouthful unless you are
sharing it with others."[22]

Mother Teresa recalled: "We had guests at table every day. At first I
used to ask: 'Who are they?' and Mother would answer: 'Some are our
relatives, but all of them are our people.' When I was older, I realized
that the strangers were poor people who had nothing and whom my
mother was feeding."[23]

What a wonderful way to present this act of hospitality. First, to put
it in terms a child could understand. Then to have the words really
explain what was going on: the welcoming of poor people to the family
table.

There was an elderly, sick, alcoholic woman, File, whose family had abandoned her. Drana would go to File every week and bring her food, bathe her, and clean her house.

Years later Drana would receive a letter from her daughter describing the fine school where she was teaching. She wrote about the fact that everyone liked her and appreciated her work.

"Do not forget," Drana wrote Teresa in reply, "that you went to India for the sake of the poor. Do you remember our File? She was covered in sores, but what caused her far more suffering was the knowledge that she was all alone in the world. We did what we could for her, but the worst thing was not the sores but the fact that her family had forgotten her."[24]

Lord, thank you for each person you have given me to love. Help me love them as you love them.

—Joel Schorn

The Foundation of Trust

Draw near to God and he will draw near to you.

—James 4:8

Our prayer life is the cornerstone for building a foundation of trust in our home. There are limits to what a husband or a wife can do; there are no limits to what God can do. In prayer, we approach our heavenly Father as his beloved daughters and sons. We give him our praise for all he is doing and our concerns for all we face and for our loved ones, for whom he has greater love than we do. Each day, we choose Christ in a kind of ongoing conversion. And each day, we choose our spouses, praying for them.

The more we grow in grace, the more we yield to the Spirit's work in our life. The Spirit produces in us "love, joy, peace, patience, kindness, goodness, faithfulness, gentleness, self-control" (Galatians 5:22–23). Rather than tackling the challenges of married life with our own strength and abilities, we ask the Spirit to give us his strength. We pray for wisdom, knowing that the Lord takes delight in "a wife and a husband who live in harmony" (Sirach 25:1).

We pray for purity, aware of temptation without being controlled by fear. Being on our guard is not the same as questioning the faithfulness of our spouses; suspicion and jealousy detract from our love. I anticipate faithfulness from me to Scott—and from Scott to me—but I also pray for faithfulness, watchful for temptations.

We also pray with thanksgiving. "Have no anxiety about anything, but in everything by prayer and supplication with thanksgiving let your requests be made known to God. And the peace of God, which passes all understanding, will keep your hearts and your minds in Christ Jesus" (Philippians 4:6–7). Anxiety accomplishes no good thing; prayer brings peace.

St. Paul emphasizes the importance of thankfulness: "Rejoice always, pray constantly, give thanks in all circumstances; for this is the will of God in Christ Jesus for you" (1 Thessalonians 5:16–18). God's will is for us to thank him always. We grow in faithfulness when we are cheerful and thankful, especially for our spouses.

Pray as a couple and as a family. Blessed Mother Teresa liked to quote Fr. Patrick Peyton's line, "The family that prays together stays together." The closer a couple gets to God, the closer they draw to each other. This is the idea behind Archbishop Fulton Sheen's teaching that it takes three to get married.[25]

Prayer keeps suffering in perspective, whether it is suffering we experience together or suffering we inflict on each other. For love of the other, we imitate Christ's embrace of the cross: "For the joy that was set before him [he] endured the cross, despising the shame" (Hebrews 12:2). We focus on the joy of what God is accomplishing in and through us in the midst of suffering.

Lord, you are the head of this house,
the unseen guest at every meal,
the silent listener to every conversation.

—*Kimberly Hahn*

❧ We Are Family! ☙

Here are my mother and my brethren! Whoever does the will
of God is my brother, and sister, and mother.

—Mark 3:34–35

The genealogy of Jesus is the family history of every Christian. Our
union with Christ through baptism draws us into the lives of those
Matthew mentions in his first chapter (see Matthew 1:1–17). We must
see our lives as the culmination of God's movement through forty-two
generations. Through the humanity of the only begotten Son, we have
a share in his divinity. God has willed from the first moment of creation
that we should be one with him forever.

The home that Mary and Joseph established in Nazareth bears the
privilege that every Christian home should have. Holiness of life is a
grace for all families who have faith in God and live in obedience to
his will. The simple lesson families can learn from Nazareth is to do
"everything in the name of the Lord Jesus" (Colossians 3:17).

We should strive each day to walk in God's ways. And we know
that his commandments are not burdensome (see 1 John 5:3), for they
correspond perfectly to our desire to love. Mutual and reciprocal self-
giving allows the Word of Christ to dwell in the home and secures each
member in "the bond of perfection" (Colossians 3:14).

Nazareth helps us see our families within the prism of God's saving
love and the trajectory of his plan of redemption. We learn to appreciate the lives that make up our home. We see what it means to subor-
dinate ourselves in love. We share in the love that led Jesus to take up
his cross and die on Calvary.

Ah! how deep was my emotion when I found myself under the same roof as the Holy Family, contemplating the walls upon which Jesus cast His sacred glance, treading the ground bedewed with the sweat of St. Joseph, under this roof where Mary had carried Jesus in her arms.[26]

—St. Thérèse of Lisieux

Lord, thank you for making me part of your own family, with the Blessed Virgin Mary and St. Joseph. With them I share in the divine communion of the Trinity. May the lifeblood of this family flow in my veins every day and show me how to share it with others.

—*Fr. Gary Caster*

Behold, how good and pleasant it is
  when brothers dwell in unity!
It is like the precious oil upon the head,

...

For there the LORD has commanded the blessing,
  life for evermore.

—PSALM 133:1–2, 3

In the midst of a conversation with my mom about home decorating, time management, and caring for loved ones, I asked, "Mom, what is the key to homemaking?" If anyone would know, it would be her.

"Relationships are at the heart of homemaking."

My mother's response surprised me. She did not recommend a resource or offer a list of principles by which she had managed a home so well for more than five decades. Instead, she explained that the art of homemaking had less to do with the tasks done inside of a house and more to do with the persons who make a house a home. Edith Schaeffer wrote: "Of course, human relationships make a house into a home: either the relationships within the house, or the welcome and understanding that guests find."[27]

Persons, not tasks, create a dwelling place. The psalmist declares, "LORD, you have been our dwelling place in all generations" (Psalm 90:1, *NRSV*). The Lord himself is our dwelling; heaven is our eternal home because he dwells there.

We express our love for God and each family member through our attention to the details of life. We accomplish our homemaking tasks in service to the significant persons in our lives. Remember: It is God—not the devil—who is in the details!

Sirach 38:24–34 mentions a number of laborers who do not have leisure to study the faith much but who are faithful to their tasks. Chapter thirty-eight concludes with this verse:

> But they keep stable the fabric of the world,
> and their prayer is in the practice of their trade. (Sirach 38:34)

This applies in such a beautiful way to all labor, especially the tasks of homemaking. Ordinary work as an expression of prayer becomes extraordinary grace.

You love your family in myriad ways throughout the day (and night!). Many of the tasks do not seem very spiritual—taking out the trash, laundering, cooking, cleaning, earning a paycheck, carpooling, helping with homework—yet every task can have a spiritual dimension, provided you do it with great love. As Mother Teresa of Calcutta reminded us, "Prayer deepens faith, and the fruit of faith is love, and the fruit of love is service, and the fruit of service is peace."[28]

You provide for the basic needs of your family as you clothe them, feed them, and shelter them in a home that is both functional and beautiful. You want to be a good steward of the time, money, and resources available to your family. In the midst of busy family life, you provide a nurturing atmosphere in which everyone can grow in holiness.

Kitchen Prayer

Lord of all pots and pans and things,
since I've not time to be a saint by doing lovely things or
watching late with Thee,
or dreaming in the dawn light or

storming Heaven's gates,
make me a saint by getting meals and
washing up the plates.
Although I must have Martha's hands,
I have a Mary mind,
and when I black the boots and shoes,
Thy sandals, Lord, I find.
I think of how they trod the earth,
what time I scrub the floor.

Accept this meditation, Lord,
I haven't time for more.
Warm all the kitchen with Thy love,
and light it with Thy peace.
Forgive me all my worrying,
and make my grumbling cease.

Thou who didst love to give men food,
in room or by the sea,
accept this service that I do.
I do it unto Thee.
—Klara Munkres

—Kimberly Hahn

COUNTING ON WOMEN: THE STORY OF ST. MADELEINE SOPHIE BARAT

He opens their ears to instruction.

—JOB 36:10

As women go, so goes the world, at least according to St. Madeleine Sophie Barat. The well-educated foundress and superior of the Society of the Sacred Heart dedicated her life to the formation of women. She believed this was the best way to bring humanity to the love of Christ.

In the ruins of the anti-Catholic French Revolution, Barat saw many people's faith also in ruins. Thanks to the influence of her brother, who later became a priest, Sophie had developed a strong faith from an early age. Thus, it pained her to see others lose their faith. Sophie passionately desired to spread the love of Jesus to the ends of the earth. As she saw it, women would be instrumental in fulfilling such a mission of charity.

She wrote, "In this century we must no longer count on men to preserve the Faith. Between women and God is often arranged the eternal salvation of husbands and sons. A woman cannot remain neutral in the world; she too is set for the fall and resurrection of many."[29]

Bold words for a woman of her day. But Madeleine wasn't afraid to be bold. She loved Jesus too much to apologize for wanting others to love him too. Her vision was grand. She had prayed to God for "*all* grace to save *all* sinners."[30] So, at age twenty, with the urging of her brother's priest friend, she and two other sisters founded the Society of the Sacred Heart to teach young women the love of God.

St. Madeleine felt that teaching future wives and mothers to love God was the key to saving as many souls as possible. She urged her teaching sisters to fill their hearts with the love of God in order to communicate that love to their pupils. And so they did.

By establishing over one hundred schools in twelve countries during her lifetime, St. Madeleine Sophie helped many young women come to know and love Jesus. And once the fire was set in their hearts, it continued to spread to others.

Lord, you are counting on me to fulfill my mission for your glory, for the love of all mankind. Open my ears to hear, and humble my heart to receive the wise instruction of others.

—Gina Loehr

Work

"We must work the works of him who sent me."

—JOHN 9:4

Let each of you look not only to his own interests, but also to the interests of others. Have this mind among yourselves, which was in Christ Jesus, who, though he was in the form of God, did not count equality with God a thing to be grasped, but emptied himself, taking the form of a servant, being born in the likeness of men. And being found in human form he humbled himself and became obedient unto death, even death on a cross. Therefore God has highly exalted him and bestowed on him the name which is above every name, that at the name of Jesus every knee should bow, in heaven and on earth and under the earth, and every tongue confess that Jesus Christ is Lord, to the glory of God the Father.

—PHILIPPIANS 2:4–11

❧ Handmaids of the Lord ❧

Behold, your mother!

—John 19:27

Writing in *Mother of the Redeemer*, Pope John Paul II says this about the call of woman in the world today:

> The figure of Mary of Nazareth sheds light on womanhood as such by the very fact that God, in the sublime event of the Incarnation of his Son, entrusted himself to the ministry, the free and active ministry of a woman. *It can thus be said that women, by looking to Mary, find in her the secret of living their femininity with dignity and of achieving their own true advancement. In the light of Mary, the Church sees in the face of women the reflection of a beauty which mirrors the loftiest sentiments of which the human heart is capable:* the self-offering totality of love; the strength that is capable of bearing the greatest sorrows; limitless fidelity and tireless devotion to work; the ability to combine penetrating intuition with words of support and encouragement.[31]

Writing more than sixty years earlier, St. Teresa Benedicta of the Cross (Edith Stein) said this about the feminine model presented by the life of the Blessed Virgin Mary:

> Were we to present the image of the purely developed character of spouse and mother as it should be according to her natural vocation, we must gaze upon the Virgin Mary. In the center of her life stands her son. She awaits His birth in

blissful expectation; she watches over His childhood; near or far, indeed, wherever He wishes, she follows Him on His way; she holds the crucified body in her arms; she carries out the will of the departed. But not as *her* action does she do all this: she is in this the Handmaid of the Lord; she fulfills that to which God has called her.[32]

Mary, our Spiritual Mother, shows us how to fulfill our call. If we are to be imbued with the Spirit of the Gospel and mirror "the loftiest sentiments of which the human heart is capable," Jesus Christ must stand in the center of our lives, and we must be handmaids of the Lord.

As explained by St. Teresa Benedicta of the Cross, "A handmaid of the Lord is imbued with the love of God, is ready to serve God according to His will, and desires to awaken and nurture the Divine Life in others."[33] These characteristics and efforts come about not through the human efforts and good intentions of the handmaid but through the gift of self-donation she makes to God, demonstrated by her complete cooperation with his divine initiative of grace.

There are three essential interior dispositions we must develop if, like the Virgin Mary, we are to be handmaids in the world today:

1. We must be receptive to the action of God;
2. We must trust in his never-failing providence in spite of circumstances; and
3. We must surrender to his holy will in all things.

In so doing, we will enter with true abandon into our call to bring life to the world and to "aid humanity in not falling."[34]

In his apostolic letter "On the Dignity and Vocation of Women," Pope John Paul II extols the vast numbers of holy women who have carried the torch of faith in apostolic service down through the ages:

In every age and in every country we find many "perfect" women who, despite persecution and discrimination, have shared in the Church's mission. Even in the face of serious social discrimination, holy women have acted "freely," strengthened by their union with Christ. Such union and freedom rooted in God explain, for example, the great work of St. Catherine of Siena in the life of the Church, and the work of St. Teresa of Jesus in monastic life. In our own days too the Church is constantly enriched by the witness of the many women who fulfill their vocation to holiness. Holy women are an incarnation of the feminine ideal; they are also a model for all Christians, a model of the *sequela Christi*, an example of how the Bride must respond with love to the love of the Bridegroom.[35]

God has chosen for us to be the "perfect" women of our day and age. If we desire to fulfill the plan of God for us, then we too must seek after holiness and desire to be *"reclothed in Christ Jesus and refreshed by His Spirit."*[36] Our hearts must be set upon the higher things—upon holiness and truth, grace and obedience, commitment and love. Thus, full of grace, we will radiate the splendor of the Bridegroom's love to his people. Each facet of our being will become a prism of God's image alive within us, reflecting a holy aura of grace and love.

In so doing, St. Teresa Benedicta of the Cross writes, we will become vessels of God's love—that is,

> an overflowing love that wants nothing for itself but bestows itself freely; mercifully, it bends down to everyone who is in need, healing the sick and awakening the dead to life, protecting, cherishing, nourishing, teaching, and forming; it

is a love that sorrows with the sorrowful and rejoices with the joyful; it serves each human being to attain the end destined for it by the Father. *In one word, it is the love of the divine Heart.*[37]

Lord, thank you for making possible for me this love, the love of your own heart! Joyfully I receive it. Let it overflow in me.

—Johnnette Benkovic

❧ PRIORITIZE YOUR PRIORITIES ❧

Not every one who says to me, "Lord, Lord," shall enter the kingdom of heaven, but he who does the will of my Father who is in heaven.

—MATTHEW 7:21

It is important for our will and desires to be aligned with God's. We are not talking here about our love of shoes or purses. (Yes, I admit I have never met a mall I did not like.) Priorities should have a purpose, and the primary purpose is to achieve a well-balanced life with God at the center of our existence.

Italy is up there in the rankings on my priority list, but Jesus is first, followed by my relationship with my husband. I have lived without God and at one point almost lost my marriage. In order to preserve both relationships, I have to work on them and not take them for granted.

If you love someone, you should want to spend time with him or her. My love for God equals time spent in prayer, reading Scripture, attending Mass, receiving the sacraments, and service. Love for my husband and respect for our marriage means being there daily, forgiving and apologizing quickly, and making the most of our time together.

Prioritizing starts with eliminating the distractions in our lives. Many people say they want to live a better life through stronger relationships with God and family, but the number of people willing to back away from distractions and help their spouses and children do the same are unfortunately few and far between. Why? Because it takes discipline and determination.

When I say "distractions," I am referring to my area of expertise: the media. You may think it is no big deal to linger online—answering your e-mails and chatting with friends on Facebook—or watch a few hours of television, but media influence is wreaking havoc in our lives. Often, the issue is the content—or the lack thereof. How can we put Jesus and our families first when the majority of the messages we see promote a "me, myself, and I" mentality, not to mention the immoral messages being beamed into our homes round the clock?

How do we think our relationships will improve when we spend more time with our laptops than our loved ones? Why do we say "Yes to the Dress" and no to one-on-one conversation? Want to strengthen your marriage? Back away from the computer.

Our Lord tells us in Matthew 6:21, "Where your treasure is, there will your heart be also." It is all about our priorities and seeing these priorities as gifts—gifts that when truly treasured will keep on giving.

Lord, you are my treasure. Please help me stay focused on the priorities you have established in my life. My deepest desires are to draw closer to you, to love the people you have given me to love, and to accomplish the mission you have for me.

—Teresa Tomeo

❧ Every Woman Is a Working Woman ❧

Whatever you do, in word or deed, do everything in the name of the Lord Jesus, giving thanks to God the Father through him.

—COLOSSIANS 3:17

The fact that the Proverbs 31 woman *works*, rather than just assigns tasks to her handmaids, highlights the fact that labor is the duty of all. Physical work ennobles us.

Before sin entered creation, Adam and Eve had tasks in the Garden of Eden, so work is not a consequence of the Fall. However, their work became much more difficult due to the consequences of sin: Adam's labor to make the land fruitful now included thorns and sweat; Eve's labor to deliver the fruit of their love included greatly increased pain in delivery (see Genesis 3:16–19).

Proverbs relates how easily someone can slip into sloth, with major consequences:

> How long will you lie there, O sluggard?
>   When will you arise from your sleep?
> A little sleep, a little slumber,
>   a little folding of the hands to rest,
> and poverty will come upon you like a vagabond,
>   and want like an armed man. (Proverbs 6:9–11)

St. Paul taught believers to work, and he gave them a good example. He expected them to continue working, even warning that anyone rejecting this teaching should be shunned, so that through shame the person would be restored to their fellowship (see 2 Thessalonians 3:6, 11–12).

Tabitha (also known as Dorcas) was a wonderful example of a woman who worked diligently with willing hands in the early Church. "She was full of good works and acts of charity" (Acts 9:36). Her heart of compassion for the widow ladies in her seaside town of Joppa led her to use her rather ordinary skill of sewing to bless them with beautiful clothes. She was equipped naturally for a supernatural work of mercy: to clothe the naked.

Many grieved when Tabitha died. Disciples preparing her for burial heard that Peter was nearby and sent two men to plead with him to see her. When Peter entered the room where Tabitha was lying, he was moved by the people's love for her and her obvious love for them, expressed in her handiwork. "All the widows stood beside him weeping, and showing coats and garments which Dorcas made while she was with them" (Acts 9:39). Her simple service had led to greatness.

Peter asked all to leave before he prayed.

> Then turning to the body he said, "Tabitha, rise." And she opened her eyes, and when she saw Peter she sat up. And he gave her his hand and lifted her up. Then calling the saints and widows he presented her alive. (Acts 9:40–41)

What were the consequences of Tabitha's resurrection? First, word spread, and many people came to faith (see Acts 9:42). Second, Peter was able to strengthen the church in Joppa, enjoying their hospitality until the Lord revealed the next phase of his mission: reaching out to gentiles (see Acts 9:43; 10:1–48). Third, Tabitha continued her diligent service for the Lord in sewing, willing to wait for heaven until the Lord no longer needed her service on earth. Her simple deeds and heart of service produced a powerful witness.

Lord, in every task of my day, help me be mindful of your call to selfless service. Let me serve others as I would serve you.

—*Kimberly Hahn*

❧ Nothing Packed in Plastic, Please ❧

O righteous Father, the world has not known thee, but I have
known thee; and these know that thou hast sent me. I made
known to them thy name, and I will make it known, that the
love with which thou hast loved me may be in them, and I in
them.

—John 17:25–26

We should pursue our dreams. We should attempt the heights we were
born to climb. We should want good things for our families and loved
ones. But when does all our pursuing, acquiring, and striving become
merely "chasing after the wind," as Ecclesiastes 4:4 (*NRSV*) describes
meaningless labor? How do we recognize the boundary between the
life goals we were meant to achieve and goals that chase the wind?

St. Paul instructs us in the fine points of doing this in Romans 12:2:
"Do not be conformed to this world but be transformed by the renewal
of your mind, that you may prove what is the will of God, what is good
and acceptable and perfect." If we haven't figured it out by reading the
life and times of Jesus Christ in the Gospels, St. Paul tells it like it is in
his letter to the Romans: being a Christian is being radically different
from the world at large. To be a Christian means to stop conforming
and start transforming our lives.

Where the world offers us a million self-help books, we should first
buy, study, read, and digest the wisdom of the Bible and the *Catechism
of the Catholic Church*. Scripture and the *Catechism* are our signposts,
pointing the way to God's good, perfect, and pleasing will for us.
Scripture and the *Catechism* are our escorts to and through the essential

truths of the Catholic faith. Before needing a therapist or a recovery group, we should preemptively get God's help with our problems by attending Mass, going to regular confession, and establishing a time to read our Bible and pray daily.

Hebrews 4:12 says: "For the word of God [Scripture] is living and active, sharper than any two-edged sword, piercing to the division of soul and spirit, of joints and marrow, and discerning the thoughts and intentions of the heart." Scripture is powerful. Scripture will help us know when we have crossed the line between the life goals we were meant to achieve and merely chasing after the wind.

Our spiritual hunger will not be satisfied and our souls will not be saved by the acquisition of anything packed in plastic. Only by accepting the gift of faith from the Lord Jesus Christ will our souls be satisfied and saved, and that gift is free for the asking.

Lord, help me discern what is of you and what is of the world, what you want me to pursue and what I should forsake, what you want me to cherish and what I should ignore. For you alone are my Savior. All my hope is in you.

—*Heidi Bratton*

❧ With Willing Hands ❧

No one who puts his hand to the plow and looks back is fit for the kingdom of God.

—LUKE 9:62

The fact that the Proverbs 31 woman works with *willing* hands highlights her delight in her work. She has a cheerful rather than a complaining spirit about her work. The translation from Syriac says, "Her hands are active after the pleasure of her heart." This is the attitude I want to have.

Usually, homemaking tasks do not frustrate me. Sure, doing the same chores week after week can get tedious, but I have been trained by my mother to see the spiritual side of things—it is possible to rise above the mundane to see the big picture. What seems like menial work can be meaningful work.

But one day I stopped in my tracks, midway up the stairs, with a basket full of clean clothes. There it was: the same Healthtex shirt I had laundered for years. Michael had worn it, Gabriel had worn it; Hannah had not worn it (since it was too boyish), but Jeremiah had worn it. Now, week after week, I was carrying it back up the stairs after Joseph had worn it, only to have him get it dirty again!

I was caught, for a moment, in the futility of what I was doing. The laundry basket almost became too heavy to carry. I cried out, "God help me! How many times am I going to wash this shirt? What's the point of all this repetitive work?" All of a sudden I felt caught on a point of self-pity, but I really *did* want a different perspective.

Almost immediately, the thought came, *Think how many children you have been able to love, week after week, through this one little shirt.*

I paused. Though the task had not changed, I had. I realized, with gratitude, that though the work was repetitive, the work on my heart and mind was not. Through the mundane work of a homemaker, God was fashioning a home in my heart where love could be expressed in myriad acts of kindness, including laundering the same shirt, which has only recently been retired from active duty since David has outgrown it!

I was *not* caring for the shirt; I was caring *for the child* who wore the shirt. The load of laundry became light, and I carried it easily the rest of the way upstairs.

I realized that though I may be sweeping the same floor, wiping the same dishes, making the same beds, washing the same clothes, something is different—*I* am. Little by little, God is giving me more of a servant heart as I relinquish my will to his, allowing the ordinary tasks of my day to reflect the extraordinary love he has for my loved ones through me.

Through ordinary work, God gives extraordinary grace. When I cooperate with that grace, I remember, "I can do all things in him [Christ] who strengthens me" (Philippians 4:13).

Lord, thank you for the many opportunities you give me each day to love and serve you and my family. Truly, this is an honor. Make me a strong and resilient instrument of your love and devotion.

—*Kimberly Hahn*

❧ Housework and Heaven's Work ℘

How lovely is your dwelling place,
   O LORD of hosts!
My soul longs, yea, faints
   for the courts of the LORD;
my heart and flesh sing for joy
   to the living God.

Even the sparrow finds a home,
   and the swallow a nest for herself,
   where she may lay her young,
at thy altars, O LORD of hosts,
   my King and my God.
Blessed are those who dwell in thy house,
   ever singing thy praise!

—PSALM 84:1–4

Call me odd, or Type A, or whatever you want, but I like to clean and organize. Once a week, on Saturday morning, I try to persuade the family to see housework my way. I cheer them on with statements like, "Housework teaches teamwork. Housework builds character. Housework improves your health!"

Well, OK, maybe I am a bit grumpier than that with those unfortunate offspring of mine who try to sleep in, but at least I refrain from using the bullhorn until after eight o'clock.

When our children were babies, wise souls used to cajole me, "Let the house go. Your babies won't stay little forever, you know."

"Oh, yeah?" I would mutter under my breath as I kept cleaning. "And just which fairy godmother do you think is going to fly in and tidy up this place with a flick of her wand?" Letting things go was a sure-fire guarantee that a neighbor would drop by and cock an eyebrow at the mess, that I would lose an important bill or maybe even lose a kid amidst the chaos. Truthfully, if my house was undone, I was undone.

Obviously, with a household of six children and upwards of twelve pets at any one time, I needed to either adjust my expectations or put in for a vocational reassignment. My adjustment happened one day through a friend who, of course, stopped by in the middle of one of "those" days. As I madly tried to explain away the disaster, my friend simply turned me around to look at the children.

A couple of them were at the table painting. Two were building mazes for our guinea pigs in the living room out of couch cushions and Legos. Another child had a friend over and was baking cookies. As if I had just been given a new pair of glasses, I saw what my friend saw: creativity, learning, play, and the fact that people were more valuable than cleanliness and order.

That night I was inspired to create a kind of life slogan to frame and hang on my wall. I wrote:

Our Home Is a Theater Stage,
Not a Museum Display.

Like a theater production, life is well lively! Unlike a museum display, life includes people that do not always fit together nicely and events that cannot always be showcased neatly. My slogan reminds me that housework is not an end in itself. The purpose of keeping an orderly home is to help us focus on the people we live with, not to showcase either the home or the people.

Trust me, though; I have not given up my desire for order and cleanliness entirely. Housework is important because it prepares the stage for the physical, spiritual, and intellectual development of everyone who lives there. In its proper priority, housework is heaven's work.

Homemaker's Prayer

Lord, we thank thee for this sink of dirty dishes;
we have good food to eat.
Thank you for this pile of laundry;
we have nice clothes to wear.
Thank you for these unmade beds;
they were comfortable last night.
Thanks for this bathroom, complete with soggy towels,
splattered mirror, and grimy sink.
Thank you for this finger-smudged refrigerator
that needs defrosting so badly.
Thank you for this oven that absolutely must be cleaned;
it has baked many good meals over the years.
Our whole family is grateful for that tall grass that needs to be moved.
Thanks for that slamming screen door;
the children are healthy and able to run and play.
Lord, the presence of all these chores awaiting me
says that you have richly blessed this family.
I shall do them all gratefully and cheerfully. Amen.
—Author unknown

—*Heidi Bratton*

◈ THE STORY OF ST. ZITA ◈

We know that in everything God works for the good with
those who love him, who are called according to his purpose.

—ROMANS 8:28

Going to work every day is hard enough even when there is a paycheck
waiting on the other side of next Friday. Some mornings we have to
force ourselves to respond to the alarm, to get to work on time, and
then to be attentive to the day's tasks. But eventually payday arrives,
and we receive our just reward. For St. Zita, however, payday never
came.

Sent at twelve years old to work in the neighboring village of Lucca,
Italy, as a housemaid for a wealthy family, Zita was not a slave. But
her master always sent her wages back home to her poor father. Zita
worked hard, but she received nothing in return other than her keep.
Yet, she dedicated herself to her domestic duties because it was the
responsibility God had given her. She believed it was only just that she
apply herself diligently to the household tasks. That was her job, so
that's what she did.

Her wholehearted devotion to her work soon raised the ire of Zita's
fellow workers. They began to conspire against her, make fun of her,
and accuse her falsely to the master. For a time, he believed their lies
and treated Zita harshly. But through all of this nasty treatment, Zita
remained calm and was never hostile in return for the injustices piled
against her. She didn't retaliate, she didn't gossip, she didn't cease
working hard, and she didn't stop treating others with kindness. She
just kept doing her job, faithfully and diligently.

Attending daily Mass and spending her free hours in prayer strengthened Zita in the face of this oppression. She even experienced occasional ecstasies, which were the only reason she was ever late for work. But even then, her chores were sometimes miraculously completed: Once she ran back to the kitchen from the chapel to find the bread already baked with no possible explanation.

Zita also had a heart for the poor. She exercised justice toward them, often sharing what little she had to feed and clothe them, and sometimes sharing from the abundance of her rich master too!

In time, Zita's goodness was too evident to ignore. She managed to win the hearts of her fellow workers and her master. She eventually took over care of the entire household. St. Zita served her master faithfully until her death at sixty years old.

Lord, thank you for the work you give me each day. Help me imitate St. Zita's love and devotion. I offer to you all those I serve and pray that you will love them through me.

—*Gina Loehr*

❧ HOSTESS WITH THE MOSTEST ❧

Be still, and know that I am God.

—PSALM 46:10

Get-togethers with family and friends present us with the perfect opportunities to work on our "inner Mary" and our "inner Martha." I am of course alluding to the famous set of biblical sisters, Mary and Martha. It is recorded in the Gospels that Jesus visited these sisters and their brother Lazarus on more than one occasion. It is, perhaps, for this reason that, in Luke 10:38–42, Martha appears to have become so close with Jesus as to completely lose her appreciation for who he is. Instead of demonstrating awe and admiration of Jesus, Martha begins complaining about her sister, Mary.

> Martha was distracted with much serving; and she went to him and said, "Lord, do you not care that my sister has left me to serve alone? Tell her then to help me." (Luke 10:40)

Wow! Can you even imagine? To welcome the Lord Jesus into your home and immediately involve him in a sibling dispute? Well, Jesus was savvy enough not to get caught in the middle of a squabble between sisters. He answered, "Martha, Martha, you are anxious and troubled about many things; one thing is needful. Mary has chosen the good portion, which shall not be taken away from her" (verses 41–42).

Now, it has to be said that both sisters loved Jesus, and both were doing their best to serve him. As holiday hostesses, we need to have an inner Martha—a part of ourselves that is on the ball enough to do the bulk of the planning, shopping, decorating, and cooking ahead of time. Jesus did not reprimand Martha for being concerned about the details. He simply pointed out that her priorities (and therefore her timing) were a little off.

This story of family dynamics reveals the idea that true Christian hospitality is not measured in the quantity or quality of food served, the cleanliness of one's house, or the number of matching place settings and serving dishes one owns. True hospitality is measured by the amount of love offered and attention given, even if the guests are "only" our family members and close friends.

How long has it been (if ever) since we really looked at each member of our family and saw a unique individual deserving of love—not because they are always so lovable but because they are created in the image and likeness of God? Is it possible that, like Martha with Jesus, we have lost our sense of awe for our family members because we are in such close relationship with them? Could this be one reason why, instead of welcoming holidays as opportunities to slow down, catch up, and reconnect with loved ones, we often only feel overwhelmed by the impending work of playing host to them?

If we will ask God to help us see each of our family members and close friends as he sees them, I think we will be better able to embrace our inner Mary—that part of us that can just sit down and listen when our guests arrive, even if all the details of the event are not in perfect order.

Mary and Martha represent two equally important ingredients of Christian hospitality: Martha beforehand; Mary in the midst. May all of us be blessed with knowing when to call upon our inner Martha and when to send forth our inner Mary.

Lord, you are the one I host at family and friend gatherings. Help me to love as did the saintly sisters Martha and Mary, always mindful of your presence and under the guidance of your Holy Spirit.

—*Heidi Bratton*

Faith

The righteous live by their faith.

—HABAKKUK 2:4, *NRSV*

Now faith is the assurance of things hoped for, the conviction of things not seen.

—HEBREWS 11:1

❧ GOD IS OUR STRENGTH ❧

On the day I called, thou didst answer me,
my strength of soul thou didst increase.

—Psalm 138:3

One man wrote, "I know I'm not going to understand women. I'll never understand how you can take boiling hot wax, pour it onto your upper thigh, rip the hair out by the root, and still be afraid of a spider." Women have strength of which men know not; we also have weaknesses we struggle to admit.

To do God's work God's way, we prepare ourselves physically and spiritually to meet the challenges in *his* strength. We acknowledge the variety of talents, skills, abilities, energy, experience, and knowledge that God has given us. We recognize that God has designed women to desire deeper interpersonal connections, heart to heart, so that through our friendships with other women, we strengthen each other. When we utilize all of these gifts, relying on the power of the Spirit, we honor the Lord.

We use the offensive weapons of Scripture (the sword of the Spirit) and prayer. We need to learn the Word of God, study it, and memorize it so that we can meditate on it and live it well. Our model is Jesus. When Satan attacks him after his baptism by twisting Scripture out of context to tempt him, Jesus refutes him with Scripture. We need to imitate Jesus by wielding the sword of the Spirit too.

Prayer is our other offensive weapon. Prayer helps us draw on God's strength so that we do not enter spiritual conflict relying on ourselves. The evil one wants us to doubt God's presence and to mistrust God's power; prayer affirms both God's presence and his power in our lives. St. John encourages us, "Little children, you are of God, and have overcome them; for he who is in you is greater than he who is in the world" (1 John 4:4). We assault the kingdom of darkness as we intercede for ourselves and others. Prayer is powerful.

We need to remember that the battle is not between my spouse and me or my child and me. The battle is for the formation of our souls in building the kingdom of God. The battle is interior, as we yield more of ourselves to the Lord; and it is exterior, as we expose what is evil and cling to what is good. We pray for heroic virtue to be faithful to the end.

The Lord helps us to keep the big picture in mind, to discern the eternal meaning behind the challenges, joys, and sufferings we experience each day. Like the psalmist, we can say, "Blessed are the men whose strength is in thee, in whose heart are the highways to Zion" (Psalm 84:5).

When we face difficulty, our heavenly Father's strength sustains us, for "God is our refuge and strength, a very present help in trouble" (Psalm 46:1). The Lord is the one who gives us strength by arming us for spiritual warfare, preparing us for answering objections to the faith, empowering us as a kingdom of priests for faithfulness to our vocations, leading us to repentance, and equipping us to grow in diligent service to him.

Lord, increase in me the virtues of faith, hope, and love that you have given me. Help me develop the virtues of courage, fortitude, justice, and temperance. I desire to be faithful to you and to joyfully welcome you when you appear in glory.

—Kimberly Hahn

✍ Morning Prayer ✎

O come, let us sing to the LORD;
>   let us make a joyful noise to the rock of our salvation!
Let us come into his presence with thanksgiving;
>   let us make a joyful noise to him with songs of praise!
For the LORD is a great God,
>   and a great King above all gods.

—PSALM 95:1–3

The Proverbs 31 woman "rises while it is yet night and provides food for her household and tasks for her maidens" (Proverbs 31:15). Why does this woman rise early in the morning, while it is still dark? She begins her day with prayer. Like the psalmist, she says, "But I, O LORD, cry to thee; in the morning my prayer comes before thee" (Psalm 88:13); or, "I rise before dawn and cry for help; I hope in thy words" (Psalm 119:147).

So many psalms speak of rising early to greet the Lord. Morning persons have probably underlined those verses. The rest of us who are night owls may have assumed these verses applied only to naturally early risers! However, we all need to spend time with the Lord in prayer at the beginning of the day—early birds and night owls alike.

Fr. Ray Ryland, a dear friend and spiritual mentor, illustrated the importance of prayer in the morning. He compared sleep to a little death in which we lose consciousness as we relinquish our control and compared rising the next day to a little resurrection. Our prayer time reminds us of who God is, who we are, and why we are doing what we are doing.

Let me hear in the morning of thy steadfast love,
　　for in thee I put my trust.
Teach me the way I should go,
　　for to thee I lift up my soul. (Psalm 143:8)

Prayer in the morning is part of our preparation for meeting our household's needs; we need to get our bearings before we are bombarded. Time for prayer is like scuba diving in the midst of a storm; it is peaceful below the storm, if we go deep enough: "O LORD, in the morning thou doest hear my voice; in the morning I prepare a sacrifice for thee, and watch" (Psalm 5:3).

When things are very difficult, we recall all that the Lord has already done for us and that he does not change even though our circumstances do.

But this I call to mind,
　　and therefore I have hope:
The steadfast love of the LORD never ceases,
　　his mercies never come to an end;
they are new every morning;
　　great is thy faithfulness.
"The LORD is my portion," says my soul,
　　"therefore I will hope in him." (Lamentations 3:21–24)

This is not wishful thinking. This is a sure hope, a greater reality than what we can see. We need to grasp—and be grasped by—this truth first thing in the morning, to establish our day. Our confidence is in the Lord; every morning he renews his promises to us.

Lord, help me begin each day in your presence. Be my portion forever.

　　　　　　　　　　　　　　　　　　　　　　—Kimberly Hahn

You are the light of the world. A city set on a hill cannot be hidden. Nor do men light a lamp and put it under a bushel, but on a stand, and it gives light to all in the house. Let your light so shine before men, that they may see your good works and give glory to your Father who is in heaven.

—MATTHEW 5:14–16

I am a strong believer in the principle that children learn more from their parents' actions than from their words. It is a principle that I call "show-don't-tell Catholic parenting." Last year, I had an experience that drove home the truth of this principle.

On the way to a high school football game, I had to drive through an unfamiliar region of southern Massachusetts. With directions in hand, I approached a busy five-way intersection and took a guess as to which lane I should be in to go straight. I guessed incorrectly and ended up in a left-turn-only lane. I stayed in the wrong lane with my blinker on, signaling a right turn, and readied myself to jump the green light in order to still go straight. I accomplished this illegal maneuver successfully and endured only a few outraged honks.

Truthfully, it was such a minor happening in the big picture of my life that I forgot about it as soon as it was over. Then, one day about six months later, I was driving a carpool when one of the teens in the car mentioned seeing me at that football game. "Oh," I said to this teen-aged friend, "I don't remember seeing you there."

"No," this friend answered, "I drove in another friend's car, but we got lost because of you."

"What?" I quipped back, not sure how this could be true.

"Well," this teen began, "the friend who gave me a ride did not have very good directions, but on the way there I saw your car and told her to follow you because you would know the way. But when we got to that big intersection—you remember, the one with the five different streets—well, we had to turn left when you cut off those cars and went straight. It was pretty dark by the time we found our way back to the game."

"We remember that!" my own children chimed in as bells started ringing in my head, and I humbly said, "Ah, yes. That intersection. Now I remember."

I hadn't meant to mislead these teens. I was more than fifty miles from home and not even aware that they were following me. But following they were, and they got lost because of me. After apologizing to this friend, three principles of show-don't-tell Catholic parenting were embossed on my mind:

- Even when we don't know it, our children—and perhaps their friends—are watching us.
- Even if we are miles away from home, alone, or unseen, there is no such thing as taking a vacation from being Catholic. (Not long after the carpool conversation, I hit the confessional about my illegal maneuver and causing the teens to get lost.)
- Most important, much more significant than showing our children the way to a football game is showing them the way to our Father in heaven. We cannot just talk about it; we must do it, too!

In John 14:6–7, Jesus tells his disciples about the way to the Father: "I am the way, and the truth, and the life; no one comes to the Father, but by me. If you had known me, you would have known my Father also; henceforth you know him and have seen him." Like Jesus with his disciples, it is through us that our children first come to know what God is like.

Without a doubt, show-don't-tell Catholic parenting is an enormous undertaking. We need God's help to do it. With God's assistance, we can begin to see that how we talk to one another, what we watch on TV or at the movies, how we use the Internet, and who we associate with when we are not at home all affect who we are and how clearly or how faintly God's face is seen through our own. With God's help, we must strive to be people of integrity. We must strive to behave in the same way when we are away from our families as we do when we are with them. And, yes, even when we are driving, we must show ourselves to be truly Catholic.

Lord, help me be available and willing to witness to your love and presence at every moment of the day.

—*Heidi Bratton*

✦ Firmly Rooted ✦

Blessed is the man
who walks not in the counsel of the wicked,
nor stands in the way of sinners,
nor sits in the seat of scoffers;
but his delight is in the law of the LORD,
and on his law he meditates day and night.
He is like a tree
planted by streams of water,
that yields its fruit in its season,
and its leaf does not wither.
In all that he does, he prospers.
The wicked are not so,
but are like chaff which the wind drives away.

—PSALM 1:1–4

The psalmist paints two vivid pictures: a mammoth tree with deep roots in the earth, which receives water constantly from the flowing stream alongside it; and wind-driven chaff, which is the refuse of good wheat—when the wheat is thrown into the air (which is still done in some third-world countries), the good seed falls to the ground and the worthless chaff blows away. We want to be like the fruitful trees planted by streams of water. And the key to having deep roots, according to the psalmist, is delighting in God's Word, reading it and meditating on it.

Rain from heaven, which causes seed to sprout, parallels God's Word, which accomplishes its work in us:

For as the rain and the snow come down from heaven,
    and return not thither but water the earth,
making it bring forth and sprout,
    …
so shall my word be that goes forth from my mouth;
    it shall not return to me empty,
but it shall accomplish that which I purpose,
    and prosper in the thing for which I sent it. (Isaiah 55:10–11)

God's Word produces fruit. Are we receptive? Do we cultivate it?

Lord, "thy word is a lamp to my feet and a light to my path" (Psalm 119:105). Thank you for revealing your Word to me. Help me to faithfully read it each day, to study it, to savor it, and to allow it to pierce my heart and draw me to you.

—*Kimberly Hahn*

Trust in the LORD with all your heart,
and do not rely on your own insight.
In all your ways acknowledge him,
and he will make straight your paths.
Be not wise in your own eyes;
fear the LORD, and turn away from evil.
It will be healing to your flesh
and refreshment to your bones.

—PROVERBS 3:5–8

Seeing the connection between going without and growing closer to God can be tricky. Like Naaman the Syrian in 2 Kings 5, we may hunger for wholeness but fill ourselves on things that actually prevent it.

In order to be healed of his leprosy, Naaman needs to die to his own way of doing things and submit to God. A little girl, an Israelite captured in war, helps him do this. She knows "there is a prophet in Israel" and encourages her master to go to him.

In Samaria, the prophet Elisha sends Naaman a message with the "diet" that will cleanse him: "Go and wash in the Jordan seven times, and your flesh shall be restored, and you shall be clean" (2 Kings 5:10). Regrettably, the waters of the Jordan are entirely distasteful to Namaan. He cannot see the connection between what he desires and what he has been told to do.

The people of Nazareth in Luke 4:24–30 are as fed up as was Naaman. They cannot recognize the prophet in their midst because they are filled with judgments. Theirs is a kind of impious indigestion that makes them rise up and drive Jesus away. They consider him to be too ordinary, too familiar, and too bland. They do not savor his words; they bristle at them. When Jesus compares them to their ancestors, who were too full to feast on the good things of the Lord, they rebel.

Jesus genuinely cares for his townspeople and wants them to stop eating the sumptuous foods that feed self-righteousness. He comes to those he loves, offering a new way of determining what will sustain them. He recounts the story of Naaman the Syrian in order to free the people of Nazareth from their fixed ideas of who he is. They need to look outside the comfort of what is familiar in order to see what God is doing in their midst.

The "fast" proposed by Jesus frightens the people. What they have been feeding on keeps them from hungering and thirsting for God and from seeing how far they have moved away from him. Jesus comes to arouse their hunger for God.

That is why fasting is so important: It puts us back in touch with what ultimately matters. Every twinge of hunger should remind us of God. Every pang allows us to see not only our need but also the One who can satisfy it.

Fasting is an opportunity to reflect on the difference between what is sumptuous and what is sustaining. Through it we can see God's power revealed in the most ordinary ways—a bath, a simple meal, a suggestion from a friend, an act of kindness, a little child.

I am the smallest of creatures; I know my misery and my feebleness, but I also know how much noble and good hearts love to do good.[38]

—St. Thérèse of Lisieux

Lord, I submit to your plan. Help me persevere in the path you have for me, even when I do not understand why you are leading me that way.

—*Fr. Gary Caster*

JEANNE JUGAN:
MODEL OF CHARITY

Therefore, since we are surrounded by so great a cloud of witnesses, let us also lay aside every weight, and sin which clings so closely, and let us run with perseverance the race that is set before us, looking to Jesus the pioneer and perfecter of our faith, who for the joy that was set before him endured the cross, despising the shame, and is seated at the right hand of the throne of God.

—HEBREWS 12:1–2

Jeanne Jugan got socked in the jaw for the sake of justice. She was making her daily rounds begging for alms on behalf of the elderly poor in her care. Approaching an older man who had the means to help, Jeanne presented her request. When he hit her, she replied, "Thank you; that was for me. Now please give me something for my poor."[39]

This selfless audacity marked Jeanne's efforts. She was never apologetic for trying to provide the poor with the basic necessities of food, clothing, and shelter. She felt it was only just that those with abundance should share with those in need. And so she begged and begged and begged and, in the course of twelve years, established fifteen homes for fifteen hundred impoverished elderly people and three hundred members of her order, the Little Sisters of the Poor. By her death, the number in the care of her new order had grown to four thousand.

"Little Sisters," she would encourage her companions as they went out to beg, "let us knock in God's name."[40] Jeanne believed her mission was ultimately the mission of the God of justice. So she swallowed her pride and hit the streets. "It cost me a lot to do this," she once confessed, "but I did it for God and for our dear poor."[41]

Jeanne herself had always known poverty. When her father was lost at sea, the Jugan family of nine was left to struggle in their small cottage in Brittany, France, in the chaotic wake of the French Revolution. At sixteen, Jeanne became the kitchen maid of a wealthy Christian woman who taught her by example the importance of caring for the sick and poor. By age twenty-five, after breaking the heart of a young sailor who desperately wanted to marry her, Jeanne bequeathed the best of her possessions to her sisters. She then set out to dedicate her life to God by serving the poor in the town of Saint-Servan.

Starting with two like-minded friends, Jeanne began taking poor old women into their home, at times giving up her own bed for them. As the number of poor grew, so did the number of women dedicated to this ministry. By 1854, their religious association received episcopal approval, and by 1879, the pope formally approved the congregation of the Little Sisters of the Poor.

Lord, through the intercession of St. Jeanne Jugan, I pray for the courage to persevere in charity. Help me to give generously to those in need, for they are you in distressing disguise.

St. Jeanne Jugan, pray for us.

—*Gina Loehr*

❧ THE EUCHARIST ❧

Jesus said to them, "I am the bread of life; he who comes to me shall not hunger, and he who believes in me shall never thirst."

—JOHN 6:35

Jesus came into this desert world of ours knowing that we were hungry for God and that there was nothing we could purchase for ourselves that would satisfy that hunger. God sent his only begotten Son into the world to feed us with a food of which we did not know, the Bread come down from heaven, his flesh for the life of the world.

Through his death, Jesus will definitively prove to every nation on earth that "God is love." By the sign of the cross, Jesus seeks to reassure us that God knows there is no end to our need for his love. He will never allow us to go hungry.

The one who has been sent as "expiation for our sins" (1 John 2:2) comes to us as a shepherd. He searches us out, and no matter how late it is when he finds us, he picks us up and brings us into the company of his fold (see Isaiah 40:11). Jesus leads us with great care and governs us with justice. He defends the afflicted and saves the children of the poor (see Psalm 72:2, 4).

God has sent his only begotten Son into the world in order to share with us the abundance of his everlasting life. All he asks is that we give ourselves to Jesus, no matter how meager, insufficient, or sinful we perceive ourselves to be. Jesus presents our lives to the Father. In a wonderful exchange of gifts—his life for ours and ours given to him—Jesus blesses us so that we are able to live more fully the love with which he first loved us.

The epiphany of God is the wondrous love of his only begotten Son. Jesus reveals himself in our nature so that we can more and more share his. By the power of his Spirit, he continues to gather us around himself, so that through word and sacrament we can eat and be satisfied. Through the Eucharist we share, God touches our lives and keeps his love alive within our hearts.

> You desire to nourish me with Your divine substance and yet
> I am but a poor little thing who would return to nothingness
> if Your divine glance did not give me life from one moment
> to the next.[42]
>
> —ST. THÉRÈSE OF LISIEUX

My Lord and my God! All praise to you in all the tabernacles of the world. Help me receive you worthily in the Most Holy Sacrament of the altar.

—Fr. Gary Caster

Wisdom from Above

I called upon God, and the spirit of wisdom came to me.

I preferred her to scepters and thrones,

and I accounted wealth as nothing in comparison with her.

Neither did I liken to her any priceless gem,

because all gold is but a little sand in her sight,

and silver will be accounted as clay before her.

I loved her more than health and beauty,

and I chose to have her rather than light,

Because her radiance never ceases.

—WISDOM 7:7–10

✒ The Gift of Wisdom ✒

Come, let us go up to the mountain of the LORD,
    to the house of the God of Jacob;
that he may teach us his ways
    and that we may walk in his paths.

O house of Jacob,
    come, let us walk
    in the light of the LORD.

—ISAIAH 2:3, 5

Initially, our obedience to God's signified will might be motivated by a sense of obligation, duty, or fear. But as we continue to grow in holiness, the impetus for our obedience changes from one of necessity to one of love, a desire to please the Beloved. Through this movement of heart, we dispose ourselves to receive the gift of wisdom, and as we faithfully continue to obey God's will, a holy perspective of life develops within us. The eyes of our soul, once clouded by the cataracts of sin, self-will, and lust for personal possessions, riches, or honors, are now able to see the events and circumstances of daily life with true clarity and vision.

As the Divine Life takes up residence within us, we see the world from God's perspective, and we find that everything in life is laden with supernatural value. We see that the silver and gold threads of God's grace weave the fabric of our lives and the tapestry of the world, making all creation shimmer with his holy presence. In short, our vision of the world changes from a purely sensate or natural perspective—one that is centered on self—to one that is informed by the knowledge and understanding of God, centered on divine love. This intimate and joyful knowledge of God and his mysteries, which we call *wisdom,* springs from loving conformity to the will of God.

Through the gift of wisdom, we can rejoice in the midst of trial, be prudent in the midst of joy, and be zealous in the midst of the mundane because we are infused with the understanding and knowledge of God. All events and situations can be appraised from this vantage point, and this yields a life influenced by good judgment and sound decision. The gift of wisdom enables the soul to taste the goodness of God.

Though wisdom is a gift of the Holy Spirit, there is much we can do to dispose ourselves to receive it. This process might be compared to the efforts we make in cultivating a garden.

First, we prepare the land. Just as we diligently remove all weeds from the plot of soil, so too do we weed our heart of any tendencies and attitudes that do not glorify God. This weeding is done through obedience to the laws of God and his Church.

Next, we till the soil, making it ready to receive the seed. By pursuing the evangelical counsels and acting upon inspirations of grace, the soil of our heart is softened and made receptive.

Then, we plant the seeds we need to produce the desired fruit. To yield the fruit of wisdom, we plant the seed of renewal, the seed of virtue, and the seed of holy reflection. These three seeds produce fruit in abundance.

Finally, we water our garden with the soaking rain of spiritual direction. This sweet rain of grace encourages the seedlings to grow roots—strong and deep—in the rich soil of truth. Thus does our garden produce a good and nourishing fruit that grows to maturity and can be shared with others.

Lord, plant your Word in me, that I may bear fruit for your kingdom.

—*Johnnette Benkovic*

What is man that thou art mindful of him,
and the son of man that thou dost care for him?

Yet thou hast made him little less than God,
and dost crown him with glory and honor.
Thou hast given him dominion over the works of thy hands;
thou hast put all things under his feet.

—PSALM 8:4–6

Satan's tactics never change. He lives to foster doubt and thereby distort reality. In the third chapter of the book of Genesis, he never tells Eve what to do; he simply encourages her to question God's word about "the tree in the middle of the garden" (Genesis 3:3, *NAB*). This confuses Eve. Has God really given her and Adam stewardship of creation? Using the goodness inherent in nature, Satan deceives the couple about the scope of human freedom.

Satan tries the same with Jesus in Matthew 4. Each temptation is nothing more than an attempt to use Jesus's humanity to confuse him. Questioning Jesus's power over nature raises doubts about the fullness of his divinity. Challenging God's providential care raises doubts about the goodness of Jesus's humanity. Offering Jesus all the kingdoms of the world raises doubts about whether the Father has already done so. Satan's method is blandly predictable; he cannot accept the fact that being human is not at odds with being one with God.

St. Thérèse could not be tricked by Satan because she never doubted the goodness inherent in being human. Acknowledging her "littleness," her fragile and vulnerable humanity, was never a rejection of God's handiwork. This humility enabled her to hold steadfastly to what is written in sacred Scripture: "He will give his angels charge of you to guard you in all your ways" (Psalm 91:11). Knowing herself imperfect made her rely on the perfection of God. Her limitations led her to trust more deeply in his care.

Thus, St. Thérèse saw the whole world as her own special garden. Rivers and streams, fish and birds, the clouds and stars in the sky, were all "desirable for gaining wisdom" (Genesis 3:6, *NAB*). She walked in a world that sang God's praises. Nature opened her eyes to the dignity of her humanity, not its shame.

St. Thérèse saw and experienced reality through the gracious gift of the one man Jesus Christ (see Romans 5:17). She believed that Jesus had willingly exposed himself to the perils of mankind so that mankind could be exposed to the glories of God. She never put God to the test but tested herself. Thérèse was content to continually bend her will to God's.

We can shatter the deceptions of Satan by holding fast to the righteousness of Christ, seeing that all of creation is good for guiding us to a greater knowledge of God.

> The act of humility I had just performed put the devil to flight since he had perhaps thought that I would not dare admit my temptation. My doubts left me completely.
>
> —St. Thérèse of Lisieux[43]

Lord, you have made each of us in your divine image. Open my eyes to see that image in the people you call me to serve.

—*Fr. Gary Caster*

Oh, how I love thy law!
>It is my meditation all the day.
Thy commandment makes me wiser than my enemies,
>for it is ever with me.
I have more understanding than all my teachers,
>for your testimonies are my meditation.
I understand more than the aged,
>for I keep thy precepts.
I hold back my feet from every evil way,
>in order to keep thy word.
I do not turn aside from thy ordinances,
>for thou hast taught me.
How sweet are thy words to my taste,
>sweeter than honey to my mouth!

—PSALM 119:97–103

Following after our Mother in the order of grace, we must learn to measure all of life's events, all of the circumstances and situations of the world, against God's Word and revelation. If we are to evaluate with the mind of God, we, too, must *ponder all these things in our hearts* in our daily time of prayer (see Luke 2:19, 51).

As we practice this form of prayerful reflection, we will see the hand of God moving in all of the situations of our lives—through the joyful times and through the sorrowful times. Our knowledge of God will grow, our human vision and understanding will be infused with the Divine Life, and we will gain true wisdom, insight, and spiritual judgment. Thus, like our Mother, we will invest our faith and trust in God's revelation to us *even as it is being revealed,* and with complete abandon we will cast ourselves into God's arms of love.

I recall a prayer meditation from my own life that showed me the value of pondering the events of our lives through the eyes of God— even those times of trial. Matthew 2:1–12 describes the journey of the Magi to the Christ Child. As I reflected upon this passage, my attention was drawn to the star.

The glorious star was God's own compass, which directed the wise men of the Orient—Gentiles—to the Christ Child. Clearly, they were transformed by the experience, drawn into a life-changing encounter with God's only begotten Son. They risked their own lives to protect this child, returning home by another route instead of reporting back to Herod, as the king had instructed.

As I continued to pray, I considered the "stars" in my own life: the people and circumstances God used to lead me to Jesus. Certainly my parents, who raised me in a Catholic home, were recognizable stars in my journey to Christ. So, too, my Catholic education imparted to me by the Vincentian Sisters of Charity and the Dominican Sisters. My husband, who loves me so completely, and our children, the fruit of our marriage, have been radiant stars lighting my way. Good and holy friends whose support and deep love of God also have been obvious stars, brilliant and lasting. The example of faith demonstrated so vividly by faithful religious and priests cast a starlit glow of grace upon my path.

Still other stars quickly appeared…. The sacraments glistened like diamonds in a velvet black sky. The Holy Sacrifice of the Mass shone with the brilliance of the noonday sun. Eucharist and Adoration of the Blessed Sacrament radiated with a splendor too effulgent to be viewed by the naked eye. And private prayer, that personal holy time of conversing with God, was a steady and faithful light illuminating the way to Jesus Christ.

Then I noticed other stars, too, stars that appeared murky and dull, their radiance shrouded by thick, dense fog. These stars represented the difficult moments in my life—the trials and tribulations, the times of intense sorrow and pain, torment and disappointment, misunderstanding and hurt. These were the circumstances and events I always categorized as "purification" and "testing."

Suddenly, these stars appeared more brilliant than all the rest, for in these moments the fruitful light of every other star in my life lent its radiance to lead me more deeply into the Divine Life.

Throughout the course of life, all of us experience many "stars"—people, circumstances, events, and situations—that can lead us closer to Christ. Some of these glow with heavenly illumination. Others are covered by the dark veil of tribulation. Yet, in the midst of it all, Jesus is with us, calling us to himself, waiting to lead us more deeply into the Trinitarian life.

Like the Blessed Virgin Mary, let us ponder in our hearts every circumstance, each situation, evaluating it in the light of God's love. Our holy reflection will pierce the darkness, and the radiance of God's plan for us will stream through.

Dear God, give us the vision to recognize our "stars," grace to accept them, and true praise and joy as we embrace them. Help us know your divine purpose for us, for our only desire is your holy will.

—*Johnnette Benkovic*

✎ Humility Yields Victory ✎

Let me hear what God the LORD will speak,
　for he will speak peace to his people,
　to his saints, to those who turn to him in their hearts.

　　　　　　　　　　　　　—PSALM 85:8

Two women, one from the Old Testament and one from the New, exemplify the humble heart that God desires. Hannah's song, recorded in 1 Samuel 2, and Mary's Magnificat, recorded in Luke 1, highlight what God's strength accomplishes in a heart yielded to him. In these hymns of praise, Hannah and Mary declare that the Lord exalts those who are humble, and he humbles those who are proud, arrogant, and mighty. Each understands that the child she bears is a gift not only to her but also to God's people.

Hannah prays, "My heart exults in the LORD; my strength is exalted in the LORD. The bows of the mighty are broken, but the feeble gird on strength" (1 Samuel 2:1a, 4). Mary proclaims, "For he who is mighty has done great things for me, and holy is his name. He has shown strength with his arm, he has scattered the proud in the imagination of their hearts and exalted those of low degree" (Luke 1:49, 51–52).

In both cases, the Lord grants a miracle. Hannah, who has been barren for years, conceives Samuel, who becomes the last of the judges to serve as a priest in the temple and the prophet who anoints Israel's first two kings. Mary, a virgin, conceives Jesus, the Savior of the world. Each woman responds with humility for the gift she has been given.

Things are not always what they seem. Jesus's crucifixion appears to be his moment of greatest weakness, an utter humiliation, yet this is his moment of triumph. By the strength of his arms (nailed to the cross) and the strength of his Spirit, he lays down his life for us. He delivers us from the bondage to sin, taking up his life again in resurrection and then mounting to heaven in his ascension.

Consider Mary, bereft of her beloved son, helpless to intervene. At the moment she is feeling deep agony at the death of her son, she never loses the virtue of joy. She participates in Jesus's self-offering as she offers her own suffering in union with his. She receives all of us as her children when Jesus gives her to the beloved disciple—and to each of us as beloved disciples who stand with her in the shadow of the cross—to embrace her as mother in heart and home.

St. Paul's prayer for the Ephesians applies to us today. He prays that we will know "what is the immeasurable greatness of his power in us who believe, according to the working of his great might which he accomplished in Christ when he raised him from the dead and made him sit at his right hand in the heavenly places" (Ephesians 1:19–20).

The same power that raised Christ from the dead and enthroned him at his Father's side in heaven has been given to us. The same power of the Holy Spirit, poured out at Pentecost on his people to prepare them for their mission, is ours. And the same power we see in the lives of the saints, the deep inner strength of people who reject what the world deems as power and choose to trust in the Lord instead, has been given to us.

Lord, I believe; help my unbelief (Mark 9:24).

—*Kimberly Hahn*

✒ WISDOM FROM OUR MOTHER ✒

Behold, I am the handmaid of the Lord; let it be to me according to your word.

—LUKE 1:38

Because of her "yes" to God at the moment of her Annunciation, Mary is intimately involved in the task of redemption. We read in Galatians 4:4, "But when the time had fully come, God sent forth his Son, *born of woman*" (emphasis added). Though Mary is but a creature like you and me, through her womb and from her genes came the One who is Redeemer. Mary's "yes" literally gave flesh to God's plan for salvation. She literally brought the Word of God to the world.

Though the Blessed Virgin Mary is the only person to bring Jesus Christ into the world physically, by virtue of our baptism each of us is called to bring God's word to others by proclaiming the Good News of salvation. The documents of the Second Vatican Council tell us that, as laity, we have an assignment in the mission of the whole people of God—namely, to work at the evangelization and sanctification of mankind. Pope John Paul II reminds us that "every Christian has to participate in the task of Christian formation, to feel the urgent need to evangelize—something, says St. Paul, 'that gives me no ground for boasting. For necessity is laid upon me.'"[44]

You and I together have been called to be ambassadors of Christ Jesus in the world (see 2 Corinthians 5:20). And what could be a more glorious call than to proclaim the marvelous truth of our salvation?

Let us pray with Mary her Magnificat:

My soul magnifies the Lord,

and my spirit rejoices in God my Savior,

for he has regarded the low estate of his handmaiden.

For behold, henceforth all generations will call me blessed;

for he who is mighty has done great things for me,

and holy is his name. (Luke 1:46–49)

Seat of Wisdom, pray for me. Lord, make me worthy of your glorious call.

—*Johnnette Benkovic*

Spiritual Motherhood

Come, O sons, listen to me,
I will teach you the fear of the Lord.

—Psalm 34:11

God calls man and woman, made in the image of the Creator "who loves everything that exists," to share in his providence toward other creatures; hence their responsibility for the world God has entrusted to them.

—Catechism of the Catholic Church, 373,
quoting Wisdom 11:24

❧ Skipping for Joy ◈

Rejoice always, pray constantly, give thanks in all circumstances; for this is the will of God in Christ Jesus for you.

—1 Thessalonians 5:16–18

Everywhere we went, Jordan—my youngest son—skipped.

I wanted to grip his hand, keep him in tow, but he was too busy skipping—he was too much of a jumping bean for me to hold his little hand in mine. After a while, I stopped trying to make him walk with me and simply learned to enjoy watching him skip—everywhere: taking a walk around the block on a cool spring morning, through the shopping mall, or down the corridors of the school where his big brothers were in attendance.

Looking back, I am not sure he really had skipping down pat. But that didn't matter. Sometimes it was more like three or four small hops and then a few random steps and then more hops, his arms sort of flailing about all the while; however, any onlooker would quickly see that my son's heart was clearly driving his little body to show his love, his enthusiasm, and his excitement for life.

I admit, his joyful attitude was contagious, and when I was finally able to simply get pleasure from watching him skip (versus attempting to make him stay at my side while I worried about life's important matters), I even tried it myself! Admittedly, I was no better at it than Jordan, but that wasn't the point. I promptly realized that life seemed better during those few seconds when I skipped. For a brief moment in time, all the things that had been on my mind—shopping for and making dinner, a looming writing deadline, a slew of papers to grade, a difficult phone call to make, an upcoming doctor's appointment—had no place. How interesting that those things which had seemed so overwhelming, so tiresome, suddenly felt lighter as they all but evaporated in my purposeful attempts at skipping.

Having a joyful attitude does that to a person; the spirit invigorates the flesh in such a way that the flesh is revitalized, renewed.

Of course, I am not suggesting that we adults begin skipping everywhere we go and that will make everything OK. Although I am not against everyone giving it a try now and again!

Rather, this is to point out what may already be known to us but we've forgotten for one reason or another: A good attitude toward things has the ability to give life to our weary limbs. And a good attitude that enlivens the limbs has the ability to invigorate others as well. Just the opposite of "A rotten apple can spoil the bunch."

Our joyful attitude has rippling, positive effects. It's a gift we are able to receive and to give quite freely.

A joyful attitude can drive us to fulfill our vocations more fully; it can do the same for others who have their eyes on us—whether it is our children, our close friends and extended family members, nosy neighbors, avowed enemies, complete strangers, or even harried coworkers.

Joy comes in many shapes and sizes. Some of us may be found skipping, while others may know true joy in the quiet, contemplative moments of life. Still others experience joy when their lives are filled with activities and demands that arise from the heart of their vocation—the vocation God has called them to, not what the world says they ought to be doing. There will be those who find joy in their crosses and those who joyfully give their lives to serve God in poverty and chastity. God has a special joy meant for each of us, but it arises from our passionate belief in its value and attainment.

We find true, complete, and lasting joy when we discern God's call upon our lives in our unique vocation. That is the miracle of seeking God's perfect and holy will.

A joyful attitude—however it manifests for each of us personally—says, "I know that I am a loved, wholly unique creature of God's with a special place in his heart."

The key, then, to a joyful attitude is an understanding that it comes from and exists in God, for him and his kingdom. In whatever circumstances we find ourselves, each of us will live more fully, more completely, if we have a joyful attitude. In other words, a joyful attitude isn't dependent upon our current situation. It is bigger than we are, and it's only a taste of things to come.

When we have a joyful attitude, we are expressing the reality that God is with us in all things. We recognize that God cares for us and desires that we find happiness in this world before then going on to live with him in eternity. A small slice of joy here on earth translates into magnificent joy in the world to come.

Lord, you are my joy! Thank you for creating me and loving me. Help me be more aware of the place I hold in your heart.

—*Cheryl Dickow*

❧ THE WAY TO JOY ☙

> The joy of the LORD is your strength.
>
> —NEHEMIAH 8:10

A number of studies, including one released by the Corporation for National and Community Service, found a strong connection between lending a helping hand and good health. The report showed that volunteers had, among other things, fewer incidences of heart disease, lower rates of depression, and greater longevity.[45] Bottom line: Give of yourself, and you get something in return. Sound familiar? We reap what we sow. It's the gift of a joyful attitude. We're a gift to others and to ourselves at the same time. Not a bad deal.

Joy is also a result of our outlook. Is the glass half empty or half full? Are we going to curse the darkness or light a candle? These questions, clichés though they may be, can help us restructure our way of thinking and, again, even affect our health in a good way.

Every time I see some secular statistics or data that back up what we know deep down to be true as Christians (but sometimes choose to ignore because we are skeptical or caught up in being Mr. or Mrs. Grumpy Pants), I chuckle to myself. Then it seems I can sense the Lord saying, "I won't say I told you so, but I told you so. Now snap out of it." Optimism is better for us than pessimism, and some studies go so far as to show it can even help us live longer. In September of 2011, a report published in the *Journal of Personality and Social Psychology* showed that positive thinking leads to healthier blood pressure and cholesterol levels and in some cases can extend life for several years.[46]

If you want to evangelize well, start with a big smile. Be joyful. Be kind. We're told in 1 Peter 3:15, "Always be prepared to make a defense to any one who calls you to account for the hope that is in you, yet do it with gentleness and reverence." Blessed Teresa of Calcutta said that joy is a net by which you catch souls.

One of my personal favorite quotes about turning those frowns upside down comes from the feisty St. Teresa of Avila, the first female doctor of the Church. "Lord, preserve us from sour-faced saints." No wonder she was known not only for her great teaching and mysticism but also for her dynamic, outgoing, and fun-loving personality.

Taking a positive or joyful approach does not mean you should walk around in la-la land, ignoring the problems you may have in your own life or in the world around you. However, it does mean that you won't be thrown off course every time trouble rears its ugly head and tries to toss you around like a toy boat in a giant swimming pool. This is the difference between joy and happiness. Joy is truly the gift that keeps on giving. Happiness is fleeting and much more dependent on feelings. Being joyful is a way of life.

Lord, I want joy to be my way of life. Help me in every situation to focus on love, not on myself.

—*Teresa Tomeo*

❧ Deborah's Witness ❧

Hear, O kings; give ear, O princes;
to the LORD I will sing,
I will make melody to the LORD, the God of Israel.

—JUDGES 5:3

Judge Deborah was a successful businesswoman, a fair and righteous judge, a valiant warrior, and a devoted wife. In all these things, Deborah was a joyful woman. She was animated in her daily life. In fact, she has been described as "fiery." We might say she was a woman on fire for her faith. The nature of her zeal toward life rose from her faith and trust in God in all her varied and demanding roles. She was the first judge to be identified as a prophetess, and she was the only judge to make rulings by which the people were expected to abide.

Deborah lived during a time of great chaos and strife for the Jewish people. As a result of disobedience toward God's laws, God had placed the Israelites under the stern and difficult rule of Sisera and the Canaanites. After twenty years of this oppression, God told Deborah that war against Sisera's rule was at hand.

General Barak (in some rabbinic teachings, Barak is also identified as Deborah's husband), when he heard the prophecy of the upcoming battle, declared that he would not enter war without Deborah at this side (see Judges 4). She agreed. As part of her gift of prophecy, Deborah foretold the way one of the battles would end: The death of Sisera would be at the hands of a woman.

This was to warn Barak—and us—that all glory, praise, and credit are always to go to God: "The road on which you are going will not lead to your glory, for the LORD will sell Sisera into the hand of a woman" (Judges 4:9).

Deborah's Canticle (Judges 5) is recognized as one of the most important praises to God in all of Torah—and one of the oldest known texts in Scripture. In it, Deborah joyfully recounts the war and its victory through God. Barak and Deborah are also known to have sung the Hallel, which is praise directed toward God. The Hallel is said at different times throughout the Jewish liturgical year, and it is also said at a victory over evil. The joyful praise and divine response is based upon Psalm 115:1 and Isaiah 48:11:

They said, "Not to us, O LORD, not to us, but to your name give glory."

The divine response, "For my own sake, for my own sake, I do it."

Deborah continually points out in her canticle that God is with the People of the Book throughout the war. It seems easy and correct for us to extrapolate that we each will, in our own personal journey, have some sort of war that we wage—it may be a war against illness or sadness or unemployment or addictions or any sort of trouble—but that God will be with us, he will strengthen us, and he will guide us if we remember to reach into the depths of our hearts and sing his praises.

We must remember, as Judge Deborah shows us, that keeping a joyful attitude is a wonderful way we can serve God. It is during those most difficult times that having a joyful attitude will lift us up and animate us—and permit us to rightfully praise God.

Deborah, as a prophetess, is associated with the celebration of Sukkot—which again reiterates the joyful attitude she possessed. During Sukkot, the Festival of Booths, in which the desert wanderings of the Jewish people are remembered, there is a tradition of shaking *etrog* (a citron), *lulav* (the fond of a date palm—these are the trees under which Deborah sat as she acted as judge), willow, and myrtle. This shaking of the different branches symbolically represents, among other things, the reciprocal concept that a joyful heart animates the limbs, and the limbs, in turn, restore the heart.

In her zeal to serve God, in the ways her joyful attitude gives life to all that she does, Deborah was able to be that successful businesswoman, that righteous judge, that valiant warrior, and that devoted wife. She shows us that the armor we are called to wear (see Ephesians 6:11) is meant to house the joyful attitude in which we are called to serve.

Lord, I want to daily proclaim the reality of your presence in the world by my joyful attitude. Establish me in your way of peace, confidence, and praise.

—Cheryl Dickow

We rejoice in our sufferings, knowing that suffering produces
endurance, and endurance produces character, and character
produces hope, and hope does not disappoint us, because
God's love has been poured into our hearts through the Holy
Spirit who has been given to us.

—ROMANS 5:3–5

"Guard your tongue when your husband is angry," St. Monica advised
her friends.[47] Monica was always at peace in spite of her husband's bad
temper, so other wives consulted her, seeking the key to her surprising
calm. They wanted to know her secret. The secret, as it turned out, was
simply self-control.

Monica had learned the virtue of temperance as a girl. Fond as she
was of wine, Monica developed the habit of secretly partaking of the
delights in her parents' wine cellar. Among those who noticed was a
girlfriend of hers who one day teased her, calling her a "wine-bibber,"[48]
which cut Monica to the heart. (Apparently, that was quite an insult
back in the day.) Monica took the opportunity to acknowledge her
weakness and made a resolution to change. She gave up the habit on
the spot.

Monica's newfound temperance soon came in handy. Her Christian
parents arranged her marriage to Patricius, a pagan from Tagaste,
Africa, close to Monica's own home. Her new spouse proved to be
irritable and unfaithful, but Monica did not allow herself to model his
behavior in return. To top it off, Patricius's disapproving mother lived
in the house with them. She didn't like Monica at all. She and the

household servants regularly engaged in gossip sessions at Monica's expense. Yet, the young wife remained charitable and even-tempered until she won the affections of her mother-in-law and influenced her husband's conversion to Catholicism.

In the midst of all this, Monica was busy bearing and raising three children, including her youngest son, whose wayward spirit caused his pious mother a lot of stress. As he grew up, his choices led to a life of dissolution and selfishness. Monica begged him to give up his sinful life. But he ignored her and publicly renounced the Catholic faith. Monica prayed for him all the more fervently.

Before her death, she was able to thank God for answering her prayers. Her son, St. Augustine, had come back to the faith. The words of consolation Monica had heard from a bishop proved to be true, "Go now, it is not possible that the son of so many tears should perish."[49]

St. Monica, patron of wives and mothers, please pray for me, that I might know and follow God's will in all the situations of family life. Help me persevere in prayer for my loved ones.

—Gina Loehr

❧ Mothering Matters ❧

As one whom his mother comforts, so I will comfort you.

—Isaiah 66:13

Recently, we had the supreme pleasure of being a foster home for a litter of stray kittens and their mother. Six fuzzy little bundles of gray, black, and brown stripes, the kittens were only four weeks old and still nursing when a friend asked if we could take care of them. She did not have to twist my arm very hard. Maybe only my pinky finger.

We cleared space in our mudroom for a good-sized cat bed, multiple water dishes, and two litter boxes. We purchased a few kitten toys, but they attracted the kittens' attention only briefly. What these bundles of joy really liked to do was to chase their mother's tail day in and day out.

Mommy cat took it well, but I noticed that she would occasionally creep away from her young 'uns and curl up by herself in a laundry basket full of beach towels stored on a shelf. Watching her do this, I smiled to myself, remembering the many bleary-eyed years I spent nursing babies, then handing them off to my husband and crawling back into bed to get a little more sleep.

One morning, about a week into caring for the kittens, we came into the mudroom to find one of the kittens missing. We began frantically searching for this gray-and-white fuzzball amid the cat toys, coats, boots, and canned goods also housed in our mudroom. Before long we found her, not in danger but snuggled up with her mother in the laundry basket. I smiled again at the similarity between this mommy cat, her kittens, and my own mothering experiences.

When the kids were of preschool age, I would try to wake up before they did in order to sneak in some prayer time before the day began. Without fail, the kids would wake up earlier, too—and find me. If I cleared a corner in the house to do a project, it would become their new favorite hangout. I learned very quickly that a playroom full of new toys simply could not hold a candle to Mommy's lap.

In the grand orchestra of family life, mothers are the conductors. In the construction of hearth and home, mothers are the master builders. Against that which would corrupt innocence, mothers are soldiers on the home front, the guardians and shepherdesses of childhood. To fledgling teens, climbing out on the limbs of self-sufficiency, mothers are the safety nets. To young adults, navigating the waters of autonomy, mothers are the lighthouses.

Mothering is an act of great courage and hope. Mothering is a personal investment in the future. Should we ever doubt the importance or influence of mothering, we need look no further than to Mary, the Mother of our Lord, whose simple *fiat* ushered in the possibility of redemption for the entire human race.

Tragically, from the litter of kittens we fostered, all but one died from distemper. Amazingly, the striped fuzzball that survived was the one that had sought and found her mother in the laundry basket. After two months of veterinary care, we adopted this kitten. Incredibly, one of the first things she did when we brought her home again was to race to the mudroom and jump up into her mother's laundry basket. I swallowed a lump in my throat as we watched her sniff around the beach towels, curl up in a ball, and go to sleep. Although mommy cat was gone, her mothering had left a lasting impression.

Mothering matters. Mothering makes a lasting difference. To all my mothering colleagues out there, thank you for letting love and life win out. I appreciate you.

Dear Lord, thank you for making me a mother! Please give me courage, wisdom, hope, and abundant love for those in my charge.

—*Heidi Bratton*

SISTER TERESA MARIA: A SPIRITUAL MOTHER

> When you give alms, do not let your left hand know what your
> right hand is doing, so that your alms may be in secret; and
> your Father who sees in secret will reward you.
> —MATTHEW 6:3–4

One of the greatest people I ever knew was Sr. Teresa Maria, a tiny
little Sister of Charity from Convent Station, New Jersey, who taught
in Our Lady of Victory School in Jersey City. But this sister did not
simply teach; she brought joy and peace and kindliness to everyone in
the class. Sr. Teresa Maria never got excited. She never was cross. She
smiled at us all, and we loved her.

As my year in second grade progressed, however, I gradually became
aware of something very strange about Sr. Teresa Maria, something
that sparked my curiosity. Every day after school she came out of the
convent, and she was always carrying something. It was usually a box,
although sometimes it was a tray covered with a large white napkin. She
then walked down a rather run-down street called Westside Avenue
until she came to what we used to call a tenement house, into which
she mysteriously disappeared.

I became more and more intrigued as the days passed, imagining
all sorts of reasons for these trips. Finally, one day I decided I had to
know what was going on, and I followed her from a distance. Careful
to remain unobserved and proud of my detective ability, I was certain
I was on the verge of discovering what Sister's secret visits were all

about—until she disappeared through the door of the tenement building. At that point, I stopped dead, not sure how to proceed.

After a few minutes, however, I began to form a new plan. On the street level of this building was a barber named Giuseppe. (In those days—at least as far as I was concerned—all barbers were Italian.) I realized that Giuseppe and his barbershop could be crucial in helping me solve the mystery of Sister's comings and goings, and so, armed with a dime (the price of a haircut back then), I entered the shop. Delighted to discover that the barber was every bit as talkative as I had hoped, I climbed into his chair.

As Giuseppe cut my hair, I interrogated him subtly (or at least I was trying to be subtle). Soon the old barber spilled the beans. He told me that Sister came to take care of an elderly woman who lived on the top floor, a woman who was very ill. This was excellent information, but like all great detectives, I craved firsthand knowledge.

After my haircut, I went around the building and climbed up the rickety old porch that served as a fire escape. When I finally I made it to the top floor, I still wasn't sure what I would see, but what I actually saw came as a great shock.

At that time I had seen only one movie in my life, Walt Disney's animated version of *Snow White and the Seven Dwarfs*, something my dad had taken me to when I was in the first grade. In those days before television, I thought the figures in the movie—we still called them "moving pictures"—were quite real. As you may remember, one of the characters in this film was a wicked old witch who threatened the life of Snow White. I peered through the window into a dark apartment, looking for Sister, but I didn't see her. Instead, staring directly at me, only a few inches back from the window, was the wicked witch—exactly as she had appeared in the movie!

My breath caught in my throat as our eyes met for the briefest of instants. Then I was in rapid motion, jumping off the milk box on which I had perched and running as fast as I was able. I remember knocking over empty beer bottles and a few potted tomato plants as I scrambled down the stairs, but I didn't care. I had to get out of there as quickly as my legs would carry me.

I kept on going, not stopping until I reached the church. There, completely out of breath, I dropped to my knees at the shrine of the Blessed Virgin. She looked sweetly down at me—as she still does these many decades later. I prayed with an intensity inspired by fear, because I had just encountered a witch.

Eventually, a question came into my mind: Why didn't the witch hurt Sr. Teresa? The answer came soon after the question: because Sister was kind to the witch—she was actually kind to a witch! Maybe if people were kinder to witches, I thought, they wouldn't be so bad. As I was contemplating these thoughts, words that I had never heard before came very clearly into my mind: "Become a priest."

I did not want to be a priest. My career had already been decided. I was sure I was destined to be a fireman.

The following year, I entered the third grade and a different school. Sr. Consolata, a Dominican, all in white except for her black veil, taught my class. One day she gave me a small gift, a holy card, and on it she wrote the words *Ora pro me*. When I showed it to my father, he asked me to find out why her inscription was in Latin. I asked her, and she looked me straight in the eye and said, "Because you're going to be a priest."

I still discussed this with almost no one, but by the fifth or sixth grade, in some way, it had become very obvious to me and others that the priesthood was to be my destiny, and so it has been. But for the beginnings of my vocation, I always go back to that day when I surreptitiously followed a wonderful, kindly nun as she carried food to a "wicked witch."

Sr. Teresa was present at my first Mass, and I recounted this story in my sermon. Some of the other sisters then told me that the old woman whom Sr. Teresa so faithfully cared for was very anti-Catholic and really quite unpleasant. Yet Sister cared for her for seven years because the old woman had no one else. The poor old soul could never even get herself to call her helper "Sister."

How important are the people we meet as we make our way through life—especially those who have a vital message for us. Sr. Teresa had no idea that she was giving a message to anyone. This was not her intention, but her work of charity, of kindness, her holy way of doing things, her saintliness, all had an effect on me that continues to this day. For seventy years, it has been clear to me that one of the first travelers I met as I was just beginning my journey was, in fact, a quiet saint.

Thank you, Lord, for all spiritual mothers who guide and inspire us to become the people you call us to be.

—*Benedict J. Groeschel*

Sources

All reflections were drawn from books published by Servant. To find any of these titles, please visit our catalog at www.FranciscanMedia.org.

Benkovic, Johnnette. *Full of Grace: Women and the Abundant Life*

Bratton, Heidi. *Homegrown Faith*

Caster, Fr. Gary. *The Little Way of Advent: Meditations in the Spirit of St. Thérèse of Lisieux*

———. *The Little Way of Lent: Meditations in the Spirit of St. Thérèse of Lisieux*

Costa, Anne. *Embracing Edith Stein: Wisdom for Women from St. Teresa Benedicta of the Cross*

Evevard, Tammy. *Becoming: The Woman God Made You to Be*

Groeschel, Benedict J. *Travelers Along the Way: The Men and Women Who Shaped My Life*

Hahn, Kimberly. *Chosen and Cherished: Biblical Wisdom for Your Marriage*

———. *Beloved and Blessed: Biblical Wisdom for Family Life*

———. *Graced and Gifted: Biblical Wisdom for the Homemaker's Heart*

Healy, Mary. *Men & Women Are from Eden: A Study Guide to John Paul II's Theology of the Body*

Herbeck, Debra. *Love Never Fails: 120 Reflections*

Kineke, Genevieve. *Set Free: The Authentic Catholic Woman's Guide to Forgiveness*

Loehr, Gina. *Choosing Beauty: A 30-Day Spiritual Makeover for Women*

———. *Real Women, Real Saints: Friends for Your Spiritual Journey*

Schorn, Joel. *Holy Simplicity: The Little Way of Mother Teresa, Dorothy Day & Thérèse of Lisieux*

Tomeo, Teresa, and Cheryl Dickow. *Wrapped Up: God's Ten Gifts for Women*

NOTES

1. John Paul II, *Christifidelis Laici,* Apostolic Exhortation on the Vocation and the Mission of the Lay Faithful in the Church and in the World, December 30, 1988, no. 16.
2. Second Vatican Council, *Dogmatic Constitution on the Church,* 40 in Austin Flannery, ed., *The Documents of Vatican II: The Conciliar and Post Conciliar Documents* (Northport, N.Y.: Costello, 1998), vol. 1, p. 397.
3. Rule of Benedict 31:10, in Timothy Fry, ed., *The Rule of St. Benedict in English* (Collegeville, Minn.: Liturgical, 1981), p. 55.
4. Dorothy Day, quoted in William D. Miller, *All Is Grace: The Spirituality of Dorothy Day* (Garden City, N.Y.: Doubleday, 1987), p. 20.
5. See, for example, Pope John Paul II, *Dies Domini,* Apostolic Letter on Keeping the Lord's Day Holy, May 31, 1998, no. 11: "It speaks, as it were, of God's lingering before the 'very good' work (Genesis 1:31) which his hand has wrought, in order to cast upon it *a gaze full of joyous delight.* This is a 'contemplative' gaze which does not look to new accomplishments but enjoys the beauty of what has already been achieved. It is a gaze which God casts upon all things, but in a special way upon man, the crown of creation."
6. Pope John Paul II, *The Theology of the Body: Human Love in the Divine Plan* (Boston: Pauline, 1997), p. 338.
7. Pope John Paul II, general audience of February 7, 2001.
8. Pope Paul VI, Vatican Council II Closing Speech, December 8, 1965.
9. Pope Paul VI, Vatican II Closing Speech.
10. Pope St. John Paul II, *Mulieris Dignitatem,* Apostolic Letter on the Dignity and Vocation of Women, 30, quoting *Gaudium et Spes,* 24.
11. Pope Paul VI, Vatican II Closing Speech.
12. Peter Julian Eymard, quoted in John Hardon, ed., *The Treasury of Catholic Wisdom* (San Francisco: Ignatius, 1987), p. 584.
13. Pope John Paul II said in his apostolic letter to women, n. 58 in Costa.
14. Edith Stein, n. 59 in Costa.
15. Edith Stein, n. 61 in Costa.
16. Dorothy Day, *The Long Loneliness* (San Francisco: HarperCollins, 1997), p. 215.
17. Dorothy Day, *Loaves and Fishes* (New York: Orbis, 1963), pp. 64–65.
18. Day, *Loaves and Fishes,* p. 177.
19. Mother Teresa, cited in Kathryn Spink, *Mother Teresa: A Complete Authorized Biography* (San Francisco: Harper, 1997), p. 70.
20. Mother Teresa, quoted in Spink, p. 296.
21. Mother Teresa, quoted in Spink, p. 133.

22. Spink, p. 6.
23. Mother Teresa, quoted in David Scott, *A Revolution of Love: The Meaning of Mother Teresa* (Chicago: Loyola, 2005), p. 41.
24. Quoted in Spink, pp. 19–20.
25. See Fulton J. Sheen, *Three to Get Married* (Princeton, N.J.: Scepter, 1996).
26. John Clarke, trans., *Story of a Soul: The Autobiography of St. Thérèse of Lisieux*, 3rd ed. (Washington, D.C.: ICS, 1996), p. 128.
27. Edith Schaeffer, *The Hidden Art of Homemaking* (Wheaton, Ill.: Tyndale, 1971), p. 99.
28. Blessed Mother Teresa of Calcutta, as quoted in Gwen C. Coniker, *Love ... Is Patient, ... Is Kind, ... Never Ends: A Compilation of Writings and Talks by Gwen Coniker and Those Who Knew and Loved Her* (Bloomingdale, Ohio: Apostolate for Family Consecration), p. 107.
29. Ann Ball, *Modern Saints: Their Lives and Faces, Book 2* (Rockford, Ill.: Tan, 1990), p. 97.
30. Ball, p. 94.
31. Pope John Paul II, *Mother of the Redeemer*, 46. Emphasis added.
32. Edith Stein, "Ethos of Women's Professions," from *The Collected Works of Edith Stein*, vol. 2, *Essays on Woman*, trans. Freda Mary Oben (Washington, D.C.: ICS, 1987), pp. 48–49.
33. Stein, p. 52.
34. Pope Paul VI, Vatican Council II Closing Speech.
35. Pope John Paul II, "On the Dignity and Vocation of Women," 27.
36. Pope John Paul II, *Christifidelis Laici*, 16.
37. Stein, pp. 51–52. Emphasis added.
38. *Story of a Soul*, p. 195.
39. Ball, p. 169.
40. Ball, p. 168.
41. Ball, p. 168.
42. *Story of a Soul*,
43. *Story of a Soul*, p. 166.
44. *Christifidelis Laici*, 33.
45. Health Benefits of Volunteering: A Review of Recent Research, Corporation for National and Community Service, May 2007, http://www.worldvolunteerweb.org.
46. Denise Dador, "Study: Positive Thinking Can Extend Life," KABC-TV, Los Angeles. Available at http://abclocal.go.com.
47. Joan Carroll Cruz, *Secular Saints: 250 Canonized and Beatified Lay Men, Women and Children* (Rockford, Ill.: Tan, 1989), p. 535.
48. Cruz, p. 535.
49. Cruz, p. 537.